# ARCHIVES OF
# A GHOST HUNTER

## CRAIG NEHRING

ISBN 10: 0359057713
ISBN 13: 9780359057719

# PREFACE

In our last two haunted books we talked about investigations in Wisconsin, so I have decided to write about all the other investigations that FVGH has done in different states as well. This book covers not only the investigations but also digs deep into the history of the places we investigate. We also include a more detailed look at these locations and the whole process of getting to our investigations and some of the mishaps along the way. You will see what it's like to be team member on a professional level and have fun along the way.

We investigate everything from Insane Asylums, prisons, old schools, and even a ship on the water. We also investigate one of the houses in Iowa, where the entire family was murdered in the middle of the night in 1912.

Our team, the Fox Valley Ghost Hunters started in 2010. We have a great team of gifted investigators and these are our stories. We hope you enjoy reading about our journeys. We are not trying to change the beliefs of anyone but try to offer up explanations for what's out there to what's referred to as the paranormal.

# ABOUT THE AUTHOR

**Craig Nehring is** Co-Author of *Wisconsin's Most Haunted* books. He is the founder of Fox Valley Ghost Hunters and has been on radio podcast shows around the world. He was featured in U.S. Cellular commercials in 2016. He was born in Milwaukee, Wisconsin but moved to Woodruff, Wisconsin in the early 80s. He graduated from Lakeland Union High in Minocqua in 1988. He waterskied for Plum-Skiters ski club in Sayner and Manitowish Waters Skiing Skeeters for 15 years combined. While living in the Northwoods he lived by the notorious haunted house called Summerwind where he spent time investigating in his early years. He moved to the Fox Valley in 2005 to start a career in transportation and decided to start a paranormal team in 2010. His team has been featured in magazines and newspapers around the world.

Craig Nehring

# AUTHOR'S NOTE

I want to thank all our followers and fans as well as team members who are presently on the team and members that are no longer with us that investigated on some of the articles in the book. A current list of team members can be found in the back of book.

Since starting Fox Valley Ghost Hunters in 2010, it's been a wild ride and came with many sacrifices. Our team has been involved in tours and events yearly which takes away from family functions. Even though we are a family-first team, the obligations can take a toll on all of us. We are and always will be dedicated to our clients and are usually available if a family needs our help in an emergency. I have found ghost-hunting is an addiction, and after you get involved, you don't want to stop. The thought of getting scared out of your wits is an adrenaline rush and something we look forward to. We look to the future to more investigations in Wisconsin and out of state.

This book is dedicated to the Grey Ghost Wilma
who spent countless hours sleeping next to me while I wrote

# Contents

# CHAPTER 1

# VILLISCA AX MURDER HOUSE
# VILLISCA, IOWA

The Villisca Ax Murder house was our first investigation out of state in 2011. I tell the story of how our team really got started. I was looking online for some unique places to investigate and found the murder house and put a deposit down to go and spend the night. My current team was a little thin due to most of them being family and friends of whom decided to part ways and do other things.

I set out on a mission to find some investigators, so I put some ads on Craigslist. It wasn't long till I got some responses and did some interviews and acquired some really good team members. I also ran into a friend, Jason, who was on some tours in New London with us, who was interested in joining the team. Now we had Jason, Jordan, Lori, Sarah, and Tammy. This would be the crew to head down to Villisca in a few months.

It seemed like forever, but the day arrived that we were leaving to head to Villisca. Three of us piled into Lori's Ford Windstar, and as I was backing out of her driveway heard a loud clunk come from under the van. I thought it was odd and put the gear to forward to hear another clunk and then again as I backed up. Lori assured me she had the van checked and nothing was wrong. She said, "nope, the guys at Ford checked it, and we are good to go."

So off we went and headed down to Iowa to stay the first night at a hotel called the Red Coach Inn and relax in the hot tub and pool, before going to the house the next evening where we would spend the night investigating. The other two women would be leaving after us to head down as they had to work later. It turned out to be a good thing for us. We were somewhere between Cedar Rapids and Des Moines, IA. I wasn't quite sure since there were corn fields on both sides as far as the eyes could see. I decided to pass a semi that was going quite slow, and when I got around him and moved back to the other lane, that's when something bad happened. The van revved up and nothing more, so I pulled to the side of the curb and attempted to put it in gear with no luck. The shifter on the steering wheel just went up and down like it was broken off.

We sat on the side of road and we called some tow companies who said there was a repair shop close by. Lori called the repair shop who stated it would be two weeks to get it fixed seeing it was likely the transmission. I got a hold of the two other team members who were on the road by now and we waited to get a ride from them, but when they arrived, they only had a compact car enough for two people. Long story short, we had to leave some of us with the van waiting for the tow truck. We drove to Des Moines, IA to get a rental car for Lori, who would be without a van for a few weeks. After renting the car which was an hour ahead of us, we had to come back to get the rest of the crew. We headed down toward our hotel, and by the time we got there, it was 11 p.m. We went to sleep right away from being so tired with all the bad luck on the way down.

The next morning we slept in and headed to town for some lunch. Town consisted of very little as there was actually not much of a town at all. We found a Pizza Ranch and grabbed a bite to eat. There were few hours before the investigation, so we figured we would go to downtown Villisca. When we arrived, it was like a ghost town with an old movie theater and a few little shops that were abandoned and had "For Sales" signs in the windows. We saw an antique shop that was open and was owned by the same owners of the murder house. We stepped inside to find tons of vintage bottles, cars, and artifacts; some of which were taken from the Ax house. Some old newspapers dated back to time about the murders of the people from the house, and there were copies to purchase, so we bought some. The owner greeted us and said if we wanted to head down to the house early, that a guy named Johnny Houser would meet us there. We headed over to the address given to us.

When we pulled up, the first thing that came to my mind was the Amityville Horror house, because the windows on second level looked like the iconic windows from Amityville. Already this house gave the team and I the creeps. We saw a guy standing out front as we stepped out of our cars. He introduced himself as the caretaker Johnny Houser, who I knew as an actor and a cinematographer, who has been in shows about ghost hunting, as well as a show on Villisca Ax Murder house. It was great getting a chance to meet him. He asked us if we wanted to go to the graveyard nearby before dark and take some pictures of the children's graves. We jumped at the idea and headed over to the cemetery to take some pictures. The gravestones from the whole family were there, separated by the sisters, parents, and the friends of the children that spent the night as well. After taking some pictures, we hopped back in the car to head back to the house and took a quick tour before we set up our equipment.

Graves of Lena and Ina Stillinger

We got back to the house and followed Johnny inside, who gave us a tour through the house. It looked rustic on the inside with an old cooking stove and photographs of the family that met their death so tragically. There was a feeling of sadness and desperation to try to solve the murders. The murderer was never caught. The kitchen was the first room to walk into from outside and there was a nook in one corner with some shelves with knickknacks dating back to the time period of the murders. In the kitchen, there was a set of stairs that led upstairs. The bedrooms and the attic was off the hallway near the bedrooms. The kitchen also opened up into a living room with a nice little wood furnace. The living room was small yet cozy, which had a piano in the corner. Just off the living room was another bedroom with a dresser and closet. We ventured upstairs, and the first bedroom was an open area with no door. We noted what looked like ax marks on the walls and ceiling, which was a sad reminder of what happened one night long ago. The hallway led to the attic with door that was a little smaller, and you had to crouch down to get into it. The last bedroom was at the end of the hall which had the closet that would open and close on its own. Thoughts that it would be a draft that caused it, but there was none. It was said that the kids used to play hide and seek and would hide in that closet.

It opened and closed on many TV shows, and we were hoping it would do the same for us later this evening. Johnny explained there was a basement but the only way to access it was from the front of the house. The basement was all dirt and a lot of cobwebs. I thought of putting a voice recorder down there, since we likely would not spend too much time in the basement. It is stated in the history, that the murderer may have hid in the attic or the pantry in the kitchen and waited for the family to go to bed before committing the crime. We headed back downstairs to unpack the gear and get it set up.

## The History of Villisca

In the early 1900s Villisca, Iowa, was a midwestern town of 2,500 with flourishing business and several dozen trains pulled into the station depot daily. The town name, Villisca, was said to stand for Pretty Place or Pleasant View. Unfortunately, for the citizens of this close-knit community, it will be forever plagued by the horrific deaths of eight people. The Moore Family, well-known and well-liked Villisca residents, and two overnight guests were found murdered in their beds. Little known to its residents was the possibility that their town was named, not after a "pretty place" but for the Indian word "Wallisca" which means "evil spirit."

In 1994, Darwin and Martha Linn purchased the former home and returned it to its original condition at the time of the murders, June 10, 1912. There have been films and books written, but the person or persons that committed the crime was never caught and surely took their dirty secret to the grave.

On June 9 and 10, 1912, Lena and Ina Stillinger, the daughters of Joseph and Sara Stillinger, left their home for church. They planned on having dinner with their grandmother after morning service, spending the afternoon with her, and later returning to her home to spend the night after the Children's Day program concluded. The girls, however, were invited by Katherine Moore to spend the night at the Moore home instead. The Children's Day Program, at the Presbyterian Church was an annual event and began at approximately 8:00 p.m. on. Sunday evening, June 9. According to witnesses, Sarah Moore coordinated the exercises. All of the Moore children, as well as the Stillinger girls participated. Josiah Moore sat in the congregation. The program ended at 9:30 p.m., and the Moore family, along with the Stillinger sisters, walked home from the church. They entered their home sometime between 9:45 and 10:00 p.m.

The following morning, at 5:00 a.m., Mary Peckham, the Moore's next-door neighbor stepped into her yard to hang laundry. At 7:00 a.m., she realized that not only had the Moore's not been outside nor the chores began, but that the house itself seemed unusually still. Between 7:00 and 8:00 a.m., Mary Peckham approached the house and knocked on the door. When she received no response, she attempted to open the door only to find it was locked from the inside. After letting out the Moore's chickens, Mary placed a call to Josiah's brother, Ross Moore, setting into place one of the most mismanaged murder investigations to ever be undertaken.

Based on the testimonies of Mary Peckham and those who saw the Moore's at the Children's Day Exercise, it is believed that sometime between midnight and 5:00 a.m., an unknown assailant entered the home of J.B. Moore and brutally murdered all occupants of the house with an ax.

Upon arriving at the home of his brother, Ross Moore attempted to look in a bedroom window and then knocked on the door and shouted, attempting to wake someone inside the house. When that failed, he produced his keys and found one that opened the door. Although Mrs. Peckham followed him onto the porch, she did not enter the parlor. Ross went no farther than the room off the parlor.

When he opened the bedroom door, he saw two bodies on the bed and dark stains on the bedclothes. He returned immediately to the porch and told Mrs. Peckham to call the sheriff. The two bodies in the room downstairs were Lena Stillinger, age 12 and her sister Ina, age 8, houseguests of the Moore children. The remaining members of the Moore Family were found in the upstairs bedrooms by City Marshall Hank Horton, who arrived shortly. Every person in the house had been brutally murdered, their skulls crushed as they slept. Josiah Moore, age 43, Sarah Montgomery Moore, age 39, Herman Moore, age 11, Katherine Moore, age 9, Boyd Moore, 7, and Paul Moore, 5, along with the Stillinger Sisters.

Once the murderers were discovered, the news traveled quickly in the small town. As neighbors and curious onlookers converged on the house, law enforcement officials quickly lost control of the crime scene. It is said that up to a hundred people traipsed through the house gawking at the bodies before the Villisca National Guard finally arrived around noon to cordon off the area and secure the home. The only known facts regarding the scene of the crime were:

Eight people had been bludgeoned to death, presumably with an ax left at the crime scene. It appeared all had been asleep at the time of the murders.

- Doctors estimated time of death as somewhere shortly after midnight.
- Curtains were drawn on all of the windows in the house except two, which did not have curtains. Those windows were covered with clothing belonging to the Moore's.
- All of the victim's faces were covered with the bedclothes after they were killed.
- A kerosene lamp was found at the foot of the bed of Josiah and Sarah. The chimney was off and the wick had been turned back. The chimney was found under the dresser.
- A similar lamp was found at the foot of the bed of the Stillinger girls; the chimney was also off.
- The ax was found in the room occupied by the Stillinger girls. It was bloody but an attempt had been made to wipe it off. The ax belonged to Josiah Moore.
- The ceilings in the parent's bedroom and the children's room showed gouge marks apparently made by the upswing of the ax.
- A piece of a keychain was found on the floor in the downstairs bedroom.
- A pan of bloody water was discovered on the kitchen table as well as a plate of uneaten food.
- The doors were all locked.

The bodies of Lena and Ina Stillinger were found in the downstairs bedroom off the parlor. Ina was sleeping closest to the wall with Lena on her right side. A gray coat covered her face. Lena, according to the inquest testimony of Dr. F.S. Williams, "lay as though she had kicked one foot out of her bed sideways, with one hand up under the pillow on her right side, half sideways, not clear over but just a little. Apparently she had been struck in the head and squirmed down in the bed, perhaps one-third of the way." Lena's nightgown was slid up and she was wearing no undergarments. There was a bloodstain on the inside of her right knee and what the doctors assumed was a defensive wound on her arm.

Dr. Linquist, the coroner, reported a slab of bacon on the floor in the downstairs bedroom lying near the ax. Weighing nearly 2 pounds, it was wrapped in what he thought may be a dish towel. A second slab of bacon about the same size was found in the icebox.

Linquist also made note of one of Sarah's shoes which he found on Josiah's side of the bed. The shoe was found on its side; however, it had blood inside, as well as under it. It was Linquist's assumption that the shoe had been upright when Josiah was first struck and that blood ran off the bed into the shoe. He believed the killer later returned to the bed to inflict additional blows and subsequently knocked the shoe over.

Had these murders been committed today, it is almost certain that law enforcement officials would have easily solved the crime and brought the murderer to justice. Almost 100 years later, however, the Villisca Ax Murders remain a mystery. The murderer or murderers are probably long dead, their gruesome secret buried with them. In hindsight, its easy to blame the officials at the time, for what could only be considered a gross mismanagement of what little evidence may have remained. The above information was taken from the website and not solely my wording. http://www.villiscaiowa.com

## Our Investigation

We started by setting up our DVR system to videotape certain parts of the house. One in the kitchen covering the stairs off the kitchen and the living room so we would see if anyone comes down or goes up the stairs. The second camera was in the attic facing back from the Amity type windows toward the hallway covering the whole attic. The third camera was at the top of the stairs facing the back bedroom, and the last camera pointed at the door in the bedroom where the ghosts of the children like to play hide and seek.

Jason and I were just finishing up setting up the camera in the back bedroom upstairs toward the closet door. We had not made it downstairs to hit the record button yet, when suddenly the closet door creaked open and slowly closed like someone went inside. It made my hair stand on end, thinking one of the children just went inside, but also there was a sad feeling in my stomach knowing we were not recording this. We noted that there was no air flow and no one went in or out of the door downstairs that might have caused a pressure change. We headed downstairs to meet with the rest of the team and hit the record button so if it happened again we would capture it. Of course it never did again the whole time we were there. (Maybe they were camera shy).

The closet door that opens and closes

The kitchen with the old stove for cooking

We conversed briefly in the kitchen to see where everyone wanted to go and decided to leave Sarah, Tammy, and Jason on the first floor to listen. Lori, Jordan, and I went upstairs to the room with the closet door and see if we could talk to the children. I pulled out a Ghost-Box, a device used to scan white noise to talk to ghosts in real time. We asked many questions to which came many answers. The answers are as follows:

Q – "What are your names?"
A – "Lena"

Q – "What happened to you?"
A – "Killed"

Q – "What can you tell us?"
A – "His Truck, He's Coming, Ina"

We decided to ask some more questions and try to get to the bottom of who killed all of them to see if they might give a name or to see if the killer was now stuck there to relive what he did over and over again. Jordan decided he would be the one to try to get the killer to give his name. We as a team do not provoke any spirits and we don't use Ouija boards. We try to be polite to what we want to communicate because these ghosts were once people too even if some were bad. Sometime we do ask certain questions to try to get certain answers and we can be firm in asking those questions. Jordan decided to try it this way by asking if the killer was there and to give us a name, but we got nothing. Then he said, "I don't believe you are here with us." While no one said anything back, something was about to happen that Jordan didn't expect.

The room started to get cold except for Jordan who got so hot in his private area of his body that he started to scream and had to vacate the bedroom for a little bit. I was about to turn on the Ghost-Box when we heard something hiss from where Jordan was just sitting, which left Lori and I a little shaken. Was this the ghost of the killer? Did he get upset when we didn't think he was there or just something else hanging out there from the constant teams doing weird things. I turned on the Ghost-Box and asked some questions about what had happened to Jordan and this is what we caught.

Q – "Who just messed with Jordan?"
A – "I did. I killed them."

A – "Legion, Lena, I didn't do it"

I turned off the box and looked at Lori and said, "What did that mean?" Legion means many, or in the Bible the word was given when Jesus asked what the demons name were. The rest was the little girl that was killed named Lena, and what didn't he do?. Was this someone hanging out there with the kids that just stated he didn't do that to Jordan or that he didn't do something else? We never figured that out.

After a while Jordan felt better and came back up to tell us to come down so we can regroup and switch locations. We would investigate downstairs and the two girls upstairs. I told them of our session we had and they said they heard some noises that sounded like they came from the cellar. I decided to walk around to the front of the house and take a voice recorder down to the cellar. I walked down the stairs to the basement and got this weird sense something or someone was watching me. I put the voice recorder down quickly and ran back up.

We are now in the living room, and all was quiet, almost as though the kids went to bed. We waited for about an hour with nothing happening. I called for the women to come downstairs and they noted that nothing was happening up there either. We decided to sit together at the top of the stairs on the landing that was in front of the bed in the open area; this was the same area with the ax marks on the wall. It was a little after midnight and it was quiet. Until we heard something, it was footsteps and they were coming up the stairs toward us. One step after another, and we all had goose bumps. Then the footsteps stopped at the top step. Nothing was there, just us and someone we couldn't see, which made it even more intense.

On review of video footage at the time of the footsteps, we captured a odd-looking orb that started in the living room and headed toward the kitchen and up the stairs. The orb or light that we captured was blinking dim to bright and was the only thing captured on video. Note this was the time the crime was stated to have possibly have happened, just after midnight. So was this the killer reliving the murders over and over? On his way up the stairs to the kids room stopping in front of us. Something we will never know.

The rest of the night was really quiet and Jordan and Lori were sleeping on the couch. Sarah and Tammy were up and asked if I wanted to check out the attic. I figured why not, so we headed up to the attic. It was really quiet and suddenly a blast of cold wind hit all of us followed by what sounded like fingernails on metal sliding down making an awful noise. The thing is, there was nothing metal up there, just wood floors and ceiling. Was this the killer sliding the ax down something to creep us out? Nothing more was heard in the next half hour, so we decided to call it a night and gathered all our gear and headed back to the hotel.

The next week we went over the voice recorder that I had in the basement. Sometime in the middle of the investigation, someone walked down the stairs in the basement and made the steps creak and a voice of a small male child called out, "Lena". Do the children still play in this home and hide in the cellar and the closet upstairs? Since they never got to grow up, are they forever playing games? I guess that is something we can't answer, or is it all residual from what they always used to do over and over in time?

## Villisca Revisited 2017

The Fox Valley Ghost Hunters went back to Villisca in March 2017 with two of the original members and some new faces that joined the team. On this investigation was Jodi, Jessica, Rick, Julia, Sheila, Jason, and I.

We set up the investigation for two nights so that we had more time to communicate with what was there. We stayed at the same hotel, but this time we had no car problems. Everything was going great until the evening of the investigation. We left the hotel to head over to the Ax Murder house. It was only 10 degrees outside and freezing with a strong wind blowing which made it very cold. The house was heated with some smaller units in the wall that would heat the house and cool the house.

We pulled up to the house and it looked the same as last time. We got out of the car to unpack our stuff and Johnny Houser walked on over to let us in. We didn't need the tour this time because some of us were here before. While we were bringing equipment in, it started to snow a little bit.

We all had some different ideas on what we were going to try the first night. We set up the cameras and some toys in the attic for trigger items to see if they would move. Our basecamp was in the living room close to one of the heaters in hopes it would keep us warm. We were ready to get started, so Jess and Jodi headed upstairs to the bedroom to see if anyone wanted to communicate with them. The rest of us hung out in the living room to see if we heard some noises and to monitor the video feeds from where the two women were located. I decided to go out to the front of the house and check in the basement and chat with anything that may be there. It was quiet in the basement and even colder. I didn't hang out there very long and came back inside.

The women were taking longer than normal. We headed up to check to see what they were doing. They were in the back bedroom where the closet was that the kids play hide and seek. Jodi and Jessica were talking to one of the children and the meters were going off like crazy, every time they asked a question. The meters were jumping to red continuously. Meaning that it was very close to the meter. I thought it seemed odd as the meters seemed to keep flashing even when questions were not asked. I asked if anyone had phone in their pocket because sometimes cell phones light up the K2 meters if they are on. They said they had them on airplane mode. I asked them to try turning the phones off just to be sure, so they did. After they had turned them off, the K2 meters stopped lighting up as frequently. I think that someone was in the room with them, but the more intense energy was caused by their cell phones.

We all decided to hang out together in the attic in a circle and see if we could capture anything. We had a camera in there so if something happened it would be recorded. It didn't take too long when Sheila said she felt something touch her shoulder. Julia felt the same thing, although she said it touched her hair. I heard what sounded like a scream or something come from within the attic. It wasn't until later that night on review of audio, a scream was captured, and it was that of a few girls screaming.

Attic with trigger objects

We all headed downstairs to warm up by the heater in the living room and took a break before starting back up again. It was getting colder and the heaters were not keeping up with how cold it had become outside. We thought that since heat rises we should concentrate upstairs. There was a barn out back where Jodi, Jessica, and Jason headed to. While they did that, Rick, Julia, Sheila, and I went up stairs to see if we could talk to the ghosts again.

The girls sat on the bed at the top of the stairs closest to what we believe were the ax marks, and Rick and I went into the back bedroom opposite of them. (We were sitting in the same area where we heard the footsteps when we came to visit a few years ago.) I was sitting down facing the hallway toward the stairs when I saw a dark shadow by the stairs. It blackened out any light that was coming in from the street light outside. Just then Rick and I got hit with a big draft of air. Julia and Sheila also felt the draft of cold air. Suddenly, Sheila screamed that something is standing right in front of them, but it disappeared as fast as it appeared. We listened for a little longer when a loud noise was heard on the stairs just in front of the women. The noise startled Julia and Sheila so much that when they jumped, the bed they were sitting on broke in the middle. When I checked to see if they were okay, I saw the frame rotted away in the middle which caused the bed to break. We checked out the stairs, but nothing more was heard or seen. We decided to call it a night and would return the next evening.

The final night at Villisca was even colder. While setting up, we were all huddled in front of the heater trying to warm our hands. We decided to once more concentrate on the upstairs because when we had the heater on, it would heat that area better than the main floor. I had a unique idea and had visited the toy store earlier in the day to pick up a fake ax. While our team is not into taunting the spirits, we sometimes feel that if we try to recreate what happened, that the spirits might respond differently. I did not want to do the swinging of the ax, so I passed it off to Rick. I had all the girls lay in beds in the house. Rick went from room to room, while our members pretended they were sleeping. Rick took the toy ax and swung it toward the beds. It was quiet and nothing seemed to happen, even though the women screamed while Rick was using the fake ax, recreating the night of the murders.

Jodi and Jess went downstairs to the living room to watch the monitors for a while. The rest of us stayed upstairs and went to the back bedroom. The girls stayed by the stairs to see if anything would reoccur. Sheila and Julia saw this weird, white rope lights that ran down the ceiling torward the stairs to the first floor. When I asked if they could describe the lights, they said, "It was like stars fell from the sky." Rick and I saw nothing from the back bedroom, and the lights were gone by the time we walked over to the women.

We investigated a couple more hours, but the cold was taking a toll on us, and we had a long drive the next morning. We had a great time at Villisca Ax Murder house and hope to go back when it is warmer. Our team would like to thank Johnny Houser for hanging out with us and sharing his stories of the house. The Villisca house offers tours and overnight investigations for teams or groups of people. We highly recommend checking it out.

Jason, Jodi, Jess, Julia, Sheila, Craig, and Rick (2017)

# CHAPTER 2

# ASHMORE ESTATES
# ASHMORE, ILLINOIS

Ashmore Estates before storm that blew off the roof

**I**n **2012 our** second investigation out of state took us to Ashmore Estates. We were intrigued by a poplular ghost hunting show that investigated there. Their unique evidence and experiences they had at this location pqued our interest. They told the story of a weatherman who did a report at this location. The weatherman was tossed to the ground by some unseen force.

We all headed down to a town called Mattoon, so we could stay close to Ashmore Estates. Scott Kelly was the owner of Ashmore, and I was able to book two nights at Ashmore. Our team was looking forward to our investigation here.

### The Ashmore Estates history

It was originally built in 1916 as the Cole County Poor Farm and operated till 1959. It was sold to Ashmore Estates Inc. who ran it as a psychiatric hospital. In 1964, after only five years in operation, they closed down because of debt. They reopened in 1965, but changed their focus from private to one that accepted patients from state mental institutions. By 1968, the care facility housed 49 residents and 10 afflicted with epilepsy.

Paul Swinford and Galen Martinie purchased the institution in 1976. They wanted to build a brand-new one-floor residency to house over 100 patients. The state, however, refused their plan. They invested over $250,000 into construction of a modern addition to the old building. It began in 1977 but was not finished until 1980s. Once the edition to Ashmore estates was finished and brought up to code, the future seemed brighter. In 1981, Barbara Jean Clark became the director.

In 1986, Paul Swinford had a limited partnership with a Peoria-based company to help manage the finances. The departments of public health and public aid dragged their feet over the insurance of proper licenses for nearly a year. This lead Swinford to file to close the facility. At that time, the losses exceeded 1.5 million. In the end, all residents had to be transferred to homes and Ashmore Estates closed its doors.

In 1988, a man by the name of Arthur Colclasure purchased the property for $12,500 and planned to turn it into his home, but repeated vandalism forced him to change his mind.

In Aug 2006, Scott Kelly purchased Ashmore Estates and started renovating; the building was a wreck. The windows were missing and it took weeks to clean. The Kellys offered flashlight tours of the place. They offered overnights to teams and guests.

In January 2013, it was hit by a bad storm that tore off the roof. The Coles County emergency stated that the building was damaged beyond repair. Scott Kelly sold the building at auction in 2013, to Robert Burton and Ella Richards for $12,700. They sold it to Robbin Terry for an undisclosed amount in 2014. They replaced the roof, installed bathrooms and many other renovations to make it safe again. It can no longer function as a fake haunted house, but it is used for paranormal investigations.

Prior to 1959, we should note that when it was a poor farm, many of the inmates died. They recorded 32 deaths out of 250 inmates who resided on the farm between 1870 and 1879. There was also a cemetery that contained between 60 and 100 bodies.

### The investigation of Ashmore Estates

When we arrived at Ashmore Estates, there was a trailer on the property to the right, with a fire pit and lawn chairs. We heard the trailer door open, and Scott Kelly came out to greet us. Scott Kelly, said, "Good luck, nothing much happens here." Then he went on to say the whole weatherman scenario was staged by the ghost hunting show and everything that happened was faked. We all looked at him blankly as he walked off with our $1400 for two nights. We looked at each other and figured we might as well investigate as some other teams that have been there caught some results. We looked up at the place in disgust as pigeons flew back and forth into the attic where the window panes were missing. The rest of the windows were broken or missing and a few had boards covering them. The mortar was all crumbling around the bricks and some were missing and lying next to the building. The building was in great disrepair.

We popped the trunks of our cars and pulled out the gear and headed inside. We hoped the inside would be better, but it was much worse. Wires were going everywhere with lights attached to them, as they were plugged into all different outlets. We have an electrician on the team who stated this whole building was in major code violations. However, we were there to investigate, not report him.

We ventured further in only to discover the halls were turned into a maze for a fake haunted house from October. It made walking down the halls very hard in spots, since all the walls hid the rooms we wanted to investigate. The real walls were covered in graffiti and there were holes in the ceilings with even more cords coming out. Water was on the floor from the rain. There was access to the attic from a ladder that went floor to ceiling, up through a small hole. We opted out of scaling the ladder and just wanted to get all the cameras set up and ready to go. Then we waited for the darkness to engulf the building for our first night investigation. On the investigation for the next two nights were Jay, Boone, Jason, Kerri, Katie, Sarah, Jeremy, Don, Lauralye, and myself. We were in for some fun for the next two nights.

It was dark, so we started with two groups. Five of us went to the basement and the other five to top floor. It didn't take long for stuff to start happening as we were hearing whispered voices coming from somewhere on the top floor. We were having a hard time locating the voices until we got close to the attic and we heard it again. Jay decided to head up the ladder with a camera to see if he could hear the voices again. When he got to the top floor he peered inside and saw what was whispering to us. It was hundreds of pigeons making these cooing sounds that sounded like whispers. He captured all the eyes of the birds on camera.

Jay headed down to the other side of the hall where Kerri was located. Jason and I decided to go down to the middle floor between both groups, to listen for more noises. When we got to the lower floor we were able to look from one side of the building to the opposite side. There was no door on the building. I heard a gush of wind go by my head and thought it was a bird. After turning on the light, I realized that it was a bat going back and forth down the hall. I swung at the bat with a broom as it darted past my head. Then I saw it fly up the stairs to the top floor. We both heard Kerri scream and we assumed she saw the bat and headed up that way. She explained that the bat hit her in the forehead which explained the scream. We called down to the basement to see how they were doing on the walkie-talkies. They said they heard some fluttering sounds which were proven to be bats. They had no other luck, so we took a break for a while and watched the monitors on the DVR. The cameras picked up the bats still flying back and forth.

We investigated for some time with nothing happening except for a noise that sounded like something was falling off the ceiling. When we investigated to try to find the noise, there were some paint chips and plaster lying on the floor from the ceiling. We heard what sounded like birds or a small animal in the floor, so the noise we heard was in fact the plaster from the ceiling falling down. That was pretty much all we heard the rest of the night. It was around 3 a.m. when the wind picked up outside and it was next to impossible to investigate. It sounded as though the roof was going to come off. You could hear something lift up and settle back down again. The pigeons were going insane with the wind and making more noise than before. We decided to call it a night and head back to the motel since we still had one more night to investigate.

The last night of investigation started very promising, a couple hours after dark, when we heard some yelling and screaming that we thought was coming from inside. I walked down to an open window and noticed the Kellys were having a bonfire party and making a lot of noise. I walked over to them to ask how long they were going to be there since we gave him a lot of money to investigate and wanted it to be quiet. He had stated it would only be an hour and they would take it inside.

Our team had an hour to kill, so we played a game of Sorry which was also the way we felt about being there at this moment. We played for a while when we heard the wind pick up outside and an odd noise coming from the floor above. We headed in that direction and up the stairs to the next floor. It was coming from a room and sounded again like screaming. When we entered the room, it stopped. There was a bunch of Halloween props lying around. There was a book about haunted stories lying on the floor that looked like it was made of foam. I kicked it over and the screaming began again. There were eight baby Robins in a hollow book that was a prop. There was no way we were getting any investigations done, so I took the birds outside by a tree and set them there so there would be no more birds screaming in the building. We headed back in and noticed some really dark clouds approaching. The Kellys headed indoors as well.

It didn't take long for the storm to hit and some more strong winds. We took cover in the basement of Ashmore, but the wind pushed the rain into the basement. We headed for higher ground and up to the first floor. We found a room that still had the windows intact and we waited the storm out, which only lasted an hour.

We were ready to get back to investigating. We sent the women in to see what they could capture as we were running out of ideas. They investigated for an hour before coming back to tell us they captured nothing and the only thing they heard was paint falling off the walls again. Katie felt bad for the little birds I put out by the trees and went to check on them. The rest of us checked out the yard to see if the storm did any damage. Katie came back to tell us the birds were no longer there, but a local cat was there now. I said, "Well, we won't be hearing the birds anymore." Jason came up to me and said that we should make a movie, a kind of parody of *Ghost Adventures*, doing an investigation here. I said, "We need a weatherman, and the of rest of the team could be the investigators." Now, we had a plan in mind and the three Jasons sat down and put their heads together for what to do next.

We started by having Don as the weatherman and Jason became a ghost in the hallway. I camped out on the stairs between levels, while Lauralye investigated the hallways. Kerri and Jay were the camera people. Jason Boone played one of the stars from the ghost hunting show. It took the rest of the night to make the movie which was more fun than investigating this place that had no activity. It would be about a year later that a funny video was released called *Our Ghost Adventures*. You can find that video under *Fox Valley Ghost Hunters* on YouTube.

Final thoughts on Ashmore Estates was the fact we were disappointed from the beginning with all the lies. We thought there would be activity because other teams have captured activity at this location. It's possible we just had some bad nights, but we have no desire to ever go back. I was told recently that the building is still in poor shape and seems like it will stay that way.

Jay, Jason, and Jason Boone brainstorm for video

# CHAPTER 3

# FARRAR HAUNTED SCHOOL
# MAXWELL, IOWA

Farrar haunted school is a favorite place for our team to investigate. We have been there fourteen times since 2013. We listed this as one of the most haunted schools in the midwest. We are close personal friends with the owners Nancy and Jim. We offer public events for guests to come and spend the night and investigate with us here. The investigations in this chapter will be a compilation of all our best evidence over the past years.

## The history of Farrar

In 1919, C.G. Geddes agreed to donate six acres of his farm to merge the area's one-room country school houses. The school boards voted and created the Washington Township Consolidated School District.

The cornerstone inscribed with the year 1921 was set and the dedication ceremony commenced on April 1, 1922. The schoolhouse was filled with citizens from miles around. An orchestra played on stage in the auditorium as a banquet was served to hundreds in attendance.

Not all citizens were behind the new building with its $100,000 price tag. One disgruntled citizen refused to attend the celebration calling it a, "Monument to the arrogance and vanity of the school board," with its boiler heating, electric lights, and indoor bathroom facilities.

On May 3, 2002, one last time, the band played, a banquet served the hundreds in attendance, and sadly, the 80-year-old schoolhouse closed its doors.

The old school sat empty until December 2006 when Jim and Nancy Oliver purchased the building. It became their home with hopes of slowly restoring the school to its original appearance and layout.

It quickly became apparent they were not alone. Voices, shadow people, and orbs were common. One day Nancy became unsteady on the stairs when a hand on her shoulder kept her from falling. She turned to thank her husband for the help, only to find no one there. Another time a dark distinct outline of a small boy was sighted on the well-lit stairway descending into the gymnasium. The boy appeared to be about 3' 6" tall with one foot on each step, and while holding on to the handrail. The figure stayed motionless for almost 2 seconds before disappearing.

## Visit hauntingatfarrar.com Farrar the town.

The large 17,000 square foot schoolhouse looks out of place in the small town of Farrar, Iowa. Farrar's population of no more than 30 people has been slowly shrinking for many years. The only growing population is in the 150-year-old cemetery across from the schoolhouse. Built on six acres of rural farmland, its old walls are beginning to crumble. Over the decades employees and students reported hearing voices, slamming doors, and sightings of unnatural figures walking the halls. Adults and children have passed on and have returned and relive their experiences, good and bad, in the old school.

## The Investigations

Our first investigation of this haunted school takes us back to 2013. I was looking online for places to investigate and saw this place in Iowa, called Farrar. It looked like it was a decent size and I figured I could get most of my team in there. I called the owners and talked with Nancy and we set up a date to investigate.

Our team members consisted of Jason, Boone, Jay, Kerri, Lori, Jordan, and Vanessa. The trip to Farrar was only five hours from where we lived. We pulled into town, which consisted of a church, graveyard, and the haunted school. There were a couple houses close by, but the rest was all fields. There was a long gravel driveway heading up to the school. We parked in front of the school, and when I got out, I heard this really loud buzzing noise that sounded like a hot transformer on a pole. Nancy came out of the school to greet us and told us the noise was from Cicadas. There were so many of them that the sound was constant.

Nancy gave us a tour of the school which consisted of four floors if you are counting the gym and basement area. When we walked through the front doors, and there was a set of stairs that lead up to the third floor. We walked around the stairs to the back where there was another door. This led to the second floor with hallways that went left and right. She pointed to a door just to the left where she and her husband lived, so if we needed anything, we knew where they were. The second floor to the left, led to a staircase that went all the way up to the third and fourth floors. To the right, led to a room we could use as a base area. In the base room, there was an air conditioner, refrigerator, microwave, chairs, and couches. The bedroom was big enough for my team and I to set up and sleep there.

We followed Nancy back out of the room to some stairs that went down to the gym. It was a standard gym with basketball hoops on each side. There were also two working bathrooms along the wall. She showed us to the boiler-room area that had lots of activity in the past where dark shadows had been seen and noises were heard. We peered in the room where there was an old furnace that no longer heated the school. In one corner, there was a hallway that was all cement which led to a dead end. When we looked up, there was a sewer cap that led outside. There was also another little room with some old water tanks or possibly oil tanks that gave me the creeps. It was really dark and had a funny odor.

Next, we headed up to the third and fourth floors. The third floor had some classrooms that looked like they could still be used. They were the old fashioned projectors, school-type chairs, and desks for the teacher. The rooms were marked for History, Math, and a small library which still had chalkboards. Nancy said we could write our team name on any of the chalkboards. There were also bathrooms on these floors, but not in use. The final floor was the last to check out. On that floor, there was an auditorium with a stage for plays. It was a large room, possibly where they set up chairs to watch the kids put on concerts and plays. There were a couple more classrooms and then a couple more stairs at the end of the hall that went to a small office. This was the principal's office, and from following other teams investigations here, he was not a nice guy, even as a ghost. The tour was over and time to start setting up.

While everyone was getting their gear together, I ventured around a bit more to check out how well the owners kept the place looking like a school. There were lockers against the wall; pictures of art and drawings still hung in the classrooms that were from some of the original children who went to school here. I saw a bunch of old pictures tacked up to a bulletin board that had some of the original sports teams from the 50s. There were names of the children who were on the sports teams, which made it easier to try to talk to them. I headed back down to find my team to start setting up cameras.

We set up a camera on the third floor facing the stage area. The second and third cameras were in the hallways, and the last camera was in the library, where they said there were lots of activity. We turned on all the equipment, and I sent Lori and Vanessa to the science rooms, while the rest of us headed up to the stage area.

We were up in the stage area when I started asking questions about the principal and if he put students in the corner. I said, "What would happen if I was the teacher and put you guys in the corner." Suddenly this loud growl came back from the corner of the room that scared the heck out of all of us. We could find nothing there at all, so continued our investigation. Jay and Kerri set up a flashlight on the stage to communicate with them by having them turn the light on and off and we were able to get some good responses for yes questions and no questions with the flashlight. The light stayed off for a while, so we figured they were getting bored of that trick. We knocked a couple times on the walls and something knocked back. I thought the knocks came from over by the stage, so I walked up by the stage and sat down against it. I knocked on the stage to see if we could get a knock back, and there was a loud knock on the stage right behind my back. I jumped to my feet, flipped on the light, and saw nothing. I noticed that there was a door there that led under the stage to store things. Jordan said he heard some noises in the hallway. We decided to sit in the hallway for a while and thought we heard a scream and some footsteps come from one end of the hall.

On the voice recorder we had with us we captured what sounded like a bunch of girls laughing and another voice that said "Peggy Screws". It got quiet, so we headed down to the basement where the gym and the boiler room were. We stopped to see how Lori and Vanessa were doing. They said they heard some voices in the science room but were unable to hear them clearly. I went over the voice recoder to see what was said.

Lori - "Don't be afraid"
Answer - "I got to go to bed"

Lori - "Did the teacher make you cry?"
Answer - "Boo Hoo"

There was also a random voice that said "Two Hours Kayla"

We left the two women to investigate the library and we headed down to the gym area. I stopped to go to the bathroom and while relieving myself bumped the Ghost-Box to the "on" position, long enough to hear a ghost say, keep it going. This made me laugh to think they had a sense of humor. We sat in the middle of the gym and the only light that we could see illuminated from the bathroom.

The gym was quiet, so we walked into the boiler room which was down a little hall off the side of the basketball court. There were no windows and it was pitch black inside. The hall led to a small room with another small room with some old rusty water tanks inside. The large room had the boiler to heat the school. We sat and listened and thought we heard a scream come from somewhere. We heard some scratching noises in one of the chases in the wall and figured out it was either birds or some animals that were inside. We noted this for later as the chases head up to some of the rooms in the school. We wanted to make sure if we were investigating the rooms, that if we heard this noise, we could account for it. There were no other noises heard so we headed back up to regroup with the women and took a break.

We met Lori and Vanessa in the breakroom and Vanessa looked white as a ghost. She explained that while in the library something had wrapped its arms all the way around her like a little kid giving someone a hug. Vanessa said she never felt anything like that and was visibly shaken to where she wanted to just stay in the room and not move. I decided to review the camera that I had facing them which captured a bare wall as the women had moved from the view of the camera to ask questions in a different part of the room, so nothing was captured on the camera.

Jason had left his maglight on the stage up on the third floor and asked if I would go with him to get it before we took a break.

When we got to the third floor we heard something run across the floor and a shadow darted out of one of the rooms opposite the stage. We went to that room but nothing was there. I went to grab the flashlight and noticed the flashlight was gone and nowhere to be found. He was sure he left it there which seemed odd to why it was not there. I said, "Let's go over the video quick and see if we see who picks it up." The video showed a dark mass near the stage and the flashlight literally disappears when the dark mass moves away. We were like wow something just took the flashlight and we never were able to locate it again.

We told everyone what had happened and relaxed for a while. I said I was getting tired, and we decided on one more walk through the school to see if we could hear anything. Vanessa opted to stay in the room and relax after getting a hug from a ghost earlier, and not only did she relax there but also she stayed in that room the next night and wanted nothing more to do with investigating.

Our final walk was very quiet. I rubbed my eyes from being tired and heard a noise from the room next to me as I was walking and glanced in for a moment but didn't see anything. We were all tired from the drive and decided to call it a night. We headed back down to the breakroom which had one bed in a small room in the back where Jordan had dibs on the bed which was fine with me since we had no idea how many people slept on it before us. I set up an air mattress next to the bed and had Lori next to me. The room was rather dark other than a window that peeked out onto the gym floor that I could see from the bathroom light below.

The rest of the team set up some beds and cots in the main room and Jason decided to sleep on the lazyboy. I tossed and turned for a while and almost drifted off to sleep when wham something smashed its hand down on my bed next to my head and that something was invisible. I jumped out of bed, and Jordan was up and felt it as well. He said, "Wait, it sounds like someone playing basketball in the gym." I heard it too and figured they couldn't sleep and figured we could join them. We came out of the room to see everyone was sound asleep. Jason and Kerri must have been too hot since they tossed their blankets on the floor and I almost fell over them. If they are sleeping up here, then who is playing in the gym? Jordan and I headed down to check it out and clearly it sounded like a full on basketball game. I thought I heard a buzzer, but when we rounded the corner and when we flipped on the light, we saw nothing and no more sounds were heard. I pinched myself to make sure this wasn't a dream. Nope, we were standing in the middle of the gym. The movie, *Field of Dreams*, popped into my head thinking if we play they will come, but it was still silent. We headed back upstairs to the sleeping area.

Jason and Kerri were sitting up along with the rest of the team. They asked if we were shooting hoops, and we said, "No, the ghosts had a game going on." It was the see-throughs against the shadows or something like that. It was unlike anything we ever heard before, and sounded as though it could be residue of the games they used to play in the gym. Kerri was cold because something pulled the blankets off them, and they felt them being pulled off their bed by something in the room and then heard a loud sigh.

This was a very interesting night and very little sleep but well worth it. We had a voice recorder in the room recording all night, and on review in the morning, we captured a voice saying, "Go help him." I thought maybe that was someone telling them to help pull the covers off. I also heard the basketballs bouncing in the distance from the invisible game in the gym.

We headed into town to get groceries for the day since we had one more night of investigations. We spent most of the rest of the day going over audio in the base room.

The team going over audio at Farrar

The second night came with a feeling of sorrow from one of our investigators that was hanging out in a room upstairs. She said she had started to cry for no reason as though she was feeling the sorrow of someone that was no longer alive. We have noted on other investigations where this has happened before. We heard some noises coming from one of the rooms and it sounded like loud bangs. We found it to be in the wall and along one of the chases where the night before we heard raccoons in the basement. We left the area as it was too noisy to hear much else; we headed back downstairs to check the cameras to see if we could find anything. I was watching for about an hour when I saw eyes appear on the stairs from the third floor and then another set of eyes and another. It didn't take long to see that the raccoons had made their way out of the chase in the wall and were now wandering through the building. We decided to have some of the team walk that way and make some noise. As they got closer, the coons returned to the hole in the wall and were gone. We covered up the hole so they were unable to come out again. We notified the owners about the coons so they could take care of it so the next guests don't run into them. They can be nasty if you get too close to them. The rest of the night was very quiet other than some random knocks and bangs. We went to bed since we had a long drive back home in the morning.

## Farrar the best of 14 years

On past trips to the school, we usually stayed in the room with the beds and couches but decided to sleep in the auditorium where we encountered most of the activity. I was tired, but others wanted to wander around for a little while. I stayed under the covers waiting for the rest of the team. I must have fallen asleep when I heard Ricks voice say, "Wake up, you missed all the action." I said what happened and he explained that the principal was making a lot of noise and seemed like he wasn't very happy at all. We happened to have a medium on this trip with us, and she said the principal was mad and the children were scared of him. They were screaming through the Ghost Box at them and something came after Julia, who was so scared that Brandon had to carry her outside away from the building. I said, "You must have had all the activity when I was asleep." I was thinking maybe I should go back to bed. They were thinking the same since they were up longer than me and now very tired as well.

We were all sleeping in the same area of the room. Some were still up reading and I had not yet fallen asleep when Rick said, "Oh my God, I just heard kids footsteps run into the room!" I said, I thought I heard something, but he must have been closer. I played back the voice recorder and yes the footsteps could be heard on there as well. We listened for a while but all was quiet, and I now was in dreamland. I woke up around 3 a.m. to the Rem-Pod going off on the stage, and the only way that will go off is if something is touching it. Others on the team were up now too and watching as well. It finally shut off when MJ, a newer team member screamed and ripped the covers off her. We asked her what was wrong and she explained that she felt hands around her neck and she couldn't breathe. She also said there was a shadow hanging over her but it had no face. We all felt a little uneasy now, but I was way too tired to stay up much longer.

I woke up to birds chirping and MJ was sitting up in bed. She had not slept since that had happened to her the rest of the night. I noticed others had packed up their stuff and was getting ready to leave. I woke up Rick and Julia so we could get on the road as well. It had been an interesting night but it was time to go home. MJ never rejoined the team after that and other than being friends on Facebook, she has not joined us since that night.

## I feel the earth move under my feet

It was us and our sister team called Fox Valley Ghost Hunters Two, which was a mistake to try to run a team with almost the same name. It didn't last long. Our trip to Farrar was very interesting. The night started out with Jason, Jeremy and I sitting in the hallway, and hearing loud noises and footsteps coming up and down the stairs, yet we saw nothing. We heard what sounded like things being tossed on the floor, which seems to happen there a lot. We noted that there was nothing falling from the ceiling. Where was it coming from? It was like ghost debris left nothing when tossed. We were waiting for team two to get to the school as they left later in the evening. Jodi, Tia, Dick, and Crystal got there later in the evening. We had them start out on the first floor and we were upstairs listening for noises. We heard the same stuff in the hallway when suddenly we heard a loud noise like something with some weight landed against the lockers in the hallway. We walked out into the hall and searched for what was tossed. It sounded too good to be true, almost like some metal was tossed. I noticed something on the floor and picked it up. It was a battery. I remembered it was mine. I took it out of the voice recorder downstairs and replaced it with a new one. The battery was sitting downstairs on a table near the video monitor. I said to Radio, "I think someone tossed that up here, not a ghost but a person from the other team". He said, "Are you sure and why would they do that?" I said, "I have no idea, but this sounds like it was a prank on us." I called down to them and asked them if they had tossed anything at all in our hallway and they all stated that they did not but was curious to the activity that was going on.

They joined us on the top floor in the room with the stage. We told them how this battery was tossed down the hall and bounced off a locker before coming to a halt on the floor. They couldn't believe it, so we all sat down and asked some questions to see if we could find out who threw the battery. Nothing more was heard, and the second team wanted to take a smoke break and also bring in their air mattresses, so they could pump them up and have a place to sleep.

While they were down smoking, I had Jeremy help me with a project of going over the video feeds which were pointing down the hallways. I could see on video if something was being tossed, as I said there was no way a ghost picked that up and brought it upstairs and tossed it. There are things up there to toss and the battery was not needed. I went back over the video and guess what I found? I found a hand of a real person picking the battery off the table and walking to the end of the hall out of sight along with some other members. On the camera closest to the stage area and hall, I saw a hand whip the battery down the hall. I don't tolerate people faking stuff.

I walked outside to where they were smoking and said to Jodi, do you know about a battery being tossed down the hall, and she said no again. I went back inside and up to the video monitor, and by that time Jason was down by the monitor as well and asked, "What's going on?" I said to the team that had just come in from smoking if they would like to watch the video that I captured the battery being tossed. Crystal finally said it was us that did it as a joke and this was now a few hours later. I was livid and Jason was hot as well since we pay good money to go to these places and not have this type of stuff happen. I stated that someone should have told me after they did it and not wait till I find out on my own. I was not very happy the rest of the trip but lucky for us we did away with the second team and the persons involved are gone now and have their own teams.

I tried to make the best of the trip and wanted to get some investigating in. We all headed back upstairs to investigate, and the second team had their mattresses pumped up and they sat on them, and we sat in the back of the room. It didn't take long for anything to happen. I asked if a girl was there named Peggy, and suddenly these super loud footsteps ran into the room and back out, but on their way back out they run over Dick's air mattress and the air mattress moved up into the air. He yelled out, "What the heck was that?" It was crazy and we heard a few screams come from in the hallway. I headed that direction and peeked into the bathroom and for the fun of it, I started to sing "Smokin in the Boys Room". On the replay of audio that night there was a girl screaming while I was singing. I guess she didn't like my voice. We went over the video and we captured an apparition coming out of the stage area as well as running over the air mattress. I think the ghosts were mad at the other team as well.

The next morning, I woke to Jodi saying, "Why are the lights swinging back and forth on the ceiling?" I said, "Why is the school moving back and forth." I could feel it as I was laying on the cot. It felt like I was out in the boat fishing and waves were hitting it. I jumped up and could still feel it. Jason and Jeremy felt it as well and it lasted 30 seconds. I went to the window and opened it up and all was quiet. I looked on my phone and nothing. I waited 10 minutes and looked again on my phone to see that an earthquake was felt all the way to Chicago and everyone was talking about it. We felt it in the school. I told the owner who was now waking up, but he slept through it. He went out to check the school and all was well except for one piece of mortar that fell out of a crack on the side of school, but there was no other damage to the school or anything that made it unsafe. I went out to check the video since I left it running all night. We had a good view down one of the hallways and was able to capture the wall moving back and forth for 30 seconds as well as the lockers and classroom doors bouncing back and forth. So, we all survived our first earthquake together. We thanked Jim and Nancy for a great time and packed our stuff up and headed home.

## Farrar and Away the event

The big event that our team was holding at Farrar was just days away. We had two team members that we don't see often, make the trek down from Northern Wisconsin for the big event. I packed up the car and I picked up Jennifer and Lisa on the way to the school. We arrived a night early, so we could set up the event in plenty of time before the guests arrived the next day. This also gave us a chance to investigate the school without so many guests. We set up some cameras and relaxed in the stage area. It was not long before the footsteps ventured into the room and back out again followed by odd noises in the hallway. I walked over to the hallway but they stopped when I got there. I stepped into a room across from the stage and sat down against the wall. I started to ask questions when I heard a loud breath of air right in front of me. I flipped on the flashlight but found nothing. I walked across the hall to the women sitting there and rewound the voice recorder to listen and sure enough the breath of air was on there. I took a voice recorder back to the room to see if we could pick anything up.

Sleep sounded like a great idea. I set some props up on the stage like balls and some of our equipment to see if something sets it off in the middle of the night. I was sound asleep, but Jennifer and Lisa were far from sleeping. They were cuddled up in the corner listening to the sound of lockers slam in the hallway on the second floor. They needed to make their way down to the bathroom in the gym, but holding it was a much better idea than passing the lockers on the way down. I woke up and they told me the story of how the lockers slammed for like half hour or least what seemed like it and there was no one else that was in the school. Lisa told me that while I was sleeping, there were noises on stage, footsteps, and something was rustling through my stuff by my bed. They said they were a bit creeped out. I decided to check the voice recorder in the next room. I rewound it to listen to it and caught a young girl singing in the room while we were all sleeping. The song was more of something young kids sang to boys that liked them. It went, He loves me, he loves me not, and so on. Wow, how cool was that to capture someone singing that.

Guests started to arrive around 3 p.m. and many were followers of our Facebook page. Kerri and Jay arrived slightly after the guests got there. We got the guests settled into the gym where they would spend the night closest to the bathrooms that had some lights on. After everyone got their stuff put away, we headed out to do some investigations. I had found a doll of a girl at a yard sale on the corner, down from the school and placed it in the stage area for the ghosts of the kids to play with. It didn't take long for stuff to start happening after the guests sat by the stage. There were sounds of footsteps running in and out of the room and loud knocks up on the stage. As if on cue, when I asked if the kids enjoyed the doll I had brought, meters were going off to my question. One guest had her hair pulled and saw a little girl standing in the doorway looking at us. One of my team members, Jodi, also saw the little girl who must have wanted to make an appearance to show us how overjoyed she was that we were there. We had the most interaction with guests that we have ever had and it was amazing. I was interrupted by a guest that stated that someone was walking around the property and they were concerned as the owners were asleep. I asked Jodi to take over for me, while Kerri, Jay, and I went to check to see who was outside the school. We walked outside to find some kids standing behind a shed on the far side of the school. They said they heard that they could just come into the school and walk through, which was not true. Someone had posted that this was an abandoned school and people could just walk in when they wanted to. This was not the case and someone posted that incorrectly, and I had heard from the owners this was happening a lot. I told them they had to pay if they wanted to join us, which they were not interested in and left the property. We headed back inside where Jodi told us that there was more activity since we left the room and that one of the guests had someone sit on their lap. It had been a long day; I was tired and so was most of the team, although some stayed up with the guests. I said it was free roam time so guests could go off on their own or investigate in small groups. Some of us decided to retire since there was another night yet to come.

I woke up early and heard more activity in one of the rooms while we were sleeping. One of the guests had some activity with something in the library and the ghost was touching her hand and her head. That was kind of cool since this guest had not had very much activity like that in her life which turns a skeptic into a believer. We had lots of different speakers for the day and a psychic medium was on hand to do some readings.

Night two of the investigation was met with the same amount of activity and noises coming from the halls. We would walk out into the halls and find nothing there and no source for the noises. I took a few guests with me, while Jodi continued in the stage area with the other guests. Kerri and Jay joined me in this one room that had an odd feel to it. There was a cloak room in the back and another small room with a sink. I sat by the desk and everyone else sat in the back of the room. I heard the floor creak back by the cloak room and then it creaked again like someone was walking forward toward me. Jay got up and went to that spot with the meter to discover that someone was indeed there. His meter that he had called a Mel-Meter, went off like crazy, letting us know that a ghost was there with us. We asked more questions and the meter kept lighting up. As quickly as the ghost came, it disappeared and must have left the room. It was quiet now, so we decided to take a break and head down to breakroom while some headed outside to smoke. I met with some of the guests in the breakroom that said they were in the boiler room in the basement and was startled by what sounded like a metal pipe being dragged across the floor. They flipped on their flashlights to find no such thing but heard it very clearly. That is a common thing and it happens quite a bit in that room.

We headed back upstairs and it was getting late and the guests wanted to wander off on their own, so we let them do so. I set up my cot and laid down while some of the other team members made sure all the members were okay. I fell asleep and woke up about 9 a.m. to find all but two guests still sleeping. There were tons of activity this weekend and we are looking forward to the next public event that will be held the following year. We thanked Nancy and Jim and headed back to Wisconsin.

The Fox Valley Ghost Hunters at Farrar

# CHAPTER 4

# EDINBURGH MANOR
# MONTICELLO, IOWA

Edinburgh Manor was a place I was interested in when I saw it on a list of places that others had investigated. It was not far for us as it was just on the other side of Dubuque, Iowa in a town called Scotch Grove. I talked with the owners and we set up a date for our team to come in. This was a sad investigation because one of our members, Daphne, was moving to Washington and would no longer be with us. We booked two nights to investigate and were to arrive at 5 p.m. on Friday; however, we got there too early and had some time to kill. We checked out one of the local parks in the area that has some really high hills and caves. Jeremy and I decided we would check out one of the high caves on a hill and made our decent to the top. It was a great view of the area, and while it seemed like a great idea at the time, looking down made me swallow a little hard. We climbed up pulling ourselves up on the rock, but going down was so steep that if you lost your footing, you would tumble all the way down to the bottom of the hill. Just to get down the hill we had to brace our feet against rocks and slowly slide down the hill, but we made it to the bottom.

We used up enough time to head back and check into the manor. When we arrived, we saw the owner of the manor waiting for us, so we went inside to sign waivers. As I got out of the car to do this, I could barely stand, my legs felt like jello, and I had no strength in them. Jay said that I had maxed out the muscles while coming down the hill and the muscles were now tight. He said it would take time but they will relax in a few hours. It was bad; I thought I wouldn't be able to even walk to investigate, but he was right they got better before we began investigating. The owner went over the history of Edinburgh Manor and the hotspots of the place.

## The History of Edinburgh Manor

In 1840, the land was originally deeded for courthouse purposes which was signed by President Buchanan. Shortly after the grant, the county seat changed but the commissioners kept the grant for the County Poor Farm. It was described as comfortable retreat for the lazy, able-bodied, and dependent applicants. The Poor Farm housed the poor, incurably insane, and disabled. Tenents worked for their food and shelter. They farmed agriculture and livestock. It was in operation from 1850 to 1910. There were eighty documented deaths.

In 1910, they closed its doors and was demolished. Edinburgh Manor was constructed and was finished in 1911 to house the insane, poor, and the elderly. It stayed in operation until 2010. It opened for paranormal investgations in 2012.

## The Investigation at the Manor

Our start to the investigation was anything but normal. It was about 3 p.m. and it was close to 100 degrees outside. The weather was also calling for severe thunderstorms and a possible tornado watch in the next 48 hours. The layout of the school had two floors, including an attic and basement. We walked the manor a few times to check things out before setting up cameras. The basement had the laundry facilities and the kitchen. There were hallways that went to different sections. One went all the way back to the boiler-room. We noted there was a very musty smell down there with a small mist rising off the walls. When we looked closer at the walls, they were covered in black mold, a fungus that can be very dangerous when inhaled. We said that anyone that comes into the basement needs to have masks on at all times. I was surprised that this was allowed in a building before opening it up to investigators. The last place that I had investigated that had black mold was shut down until they cleaned it up.

We headed back up to the main floor and then to the second floor. Each wing went the same direction, but when you got to each end of the building, the hallway would go right to one wing and left to another. I ended up getting turned around in one of the wings and wasn't sure what side of the building I was on. I found my way back to the other side and saw a door that went up again. I called for everyone to join me. We went up the stairs and found the attic which had one long beam going from one side of the building all the way to the other. It was wide enough to walk on, but if we were to fall off, we might go through the floor. The floor of the attic was all insulation and very little else was up there. I expected it to be filled with items, but other than a few boxes and some wiring that looked like it might be going to the antenna.

We ventured back down, as it was extremely hot in the attic. We decided to go from room to room to check them out and see where we should put cameras for the investigation. Jeremy and I said that it was weird that nobody did anything with the loose paint in the building. There were loose paint chips falling off the walls, and all the ceilings. It was just in such a poor shape, it made you wonder where all the money was going that they were getting for the overnights—definitely not into cleaning the place up. We found a room not far off the main entrance that we made into our base camp and sleeping area.

We grabbed our cameras and put one in the attic and one on the two main floors in the hallways facing down toward the rooms where the insane slept. The last camera was set up in the basement near the long hallway between the kitchen and laundry room. We were hot and it was very hard to think. I came up with an idea to stay cool. I saw some AC units in the windows of the bedrooms that looked like they were not that old. Jeremy and I went to get them and brought them back to our base room. Jay, who works in the heating and cooling field, said they should be okay to use. We placed them in each window and relaxed in there and waited for the room to cool off. Radio and Daphne set up cots on one side of the room while Jeremy and I were on the other. Jay and Kerri had this cot that converted into a covered little room that was a little cooler than the rest of us sleeping in the open area. It was still a couple hours before dark. We decided to take a nap.

I woke up to Daphne and Kerri saying that they saw a white thing swirling in the basement, on one of the cameras. We looked closer and found that with all the humidity in the basement caused the white fog to rise up off the black mold. We all looked at each other and said no one is going in the basement. The masks we had would not protect us from the mold down there. It reminded me of a movie called *The Fog.* I left the camera down there to capture anything if we were not there. We were about ready to start when I thought I heard sirens in the distance. We stepped outside, the sky was black in front of us, even more so than usual, and the lightning could be seen in the distance. The sirens that were going off were tornado sirens. We turned the radio on and found out a tornado was spotted about 5 miles away. That was followed by news of high winds to head our way. We went back inside and wasn't sure which was worse—the tornado or the mold in the basement.

We decided to wait a little bit before starting in case the weather got worse. It didn't take long for the high winds to hit. They were saying 60 to 70 mph. It lasted about 20 minutes with some hard rain. The rain slowed down, but the wind gusts would rattle the windows. It was not hot anymore and the wind was something we would have to deal with for a couple of hours. I sent Radio out to the other side of the building. Radio is a member named Jason, but since we had two Jasons there that night, I called the one Radio since he used to work at Radio Shack. I had him set up on the other side of the manor with a Walkie-Talkie. We also had a Walkie-Talkie and asked him to put his on Whisper Mode and ours as well. What that does is open a line of dead air or white noise to see if something says anything when we ask questions. Not all devices have this feature, but these did. We thought we heard something sigh or grunt on the other side by Radio. I told him I heard something and he said he didn't see anything. We tried this for a while, then Jay, Radio, Jeremy, and I headed out to investigate on our own for a bit while Daphne and Kerri stayed back to watch the cameras.

We headed up to the attic to check it out and do some recordings up there. It sounded like the wind calmed down and was not blowing as hard. We ventured across the beam in a line and stopped somewhere in the middle to ask if anyone was up there besides us. I felt a small blast of air go past my head when Jeremy flipped on his light and yelled "Bat." There were bats in the attic. We didn't stay up there long since we were in line with the flight path of these winged creatures. We headed down to the floor below the attic and we sat in one of the rooms. We heard some noises coming from some of the other rooms next to us. I suggested that we take a break and then get the rest of our team sit in a room up here and try to figure out where the noises were coming from.

We were about to head out for round two, when Greg, a friend of the team, showed up to hang out with us for the weekend. He was late due to the storms in the area. He had a long drive and wanted to kick back and relax a bit. I told him to stay by the camera and watch for anything that moves or looks out of place. We all headed to the second floor where we had heard stuff moving in the rooms. We each sat in a different room and listened. It didn't take long to start hearing the same things. Some were coming from the hall and some were in the rooms we were in. It also didn't take long to figure out what it was. It was all the loose paint on the walls and ceilings falling to the floor and some were really big pieces. How disappointing it was to think we were getting some activity only to find out it's paint chips. They say this is one of the most haunted places in Iowa, but I think it's the environment causing most of the haunting with paint chips that sounds like small footsteps or knocks. Why wouldn't the owners just go over the walls and get the loose paint off? The paint chips fell all night long and into the morning. It was hard to tell what could be paranormal. Is this a way to trick teams into thinking they are hearing stuff all around them when really they are not? We decided to get some sleep and headed back to basecamp. Greg said he wrote down a timestamp of where he thought he saw something on the camera. I looked it up on the DVR and checked that time frame out. We saw what looked like a white ball or orb of light. It is hard for us to believe in orbs as 99.9 percent of the time its dust or pollen in the air. However, this one seemed like it came out of a room, down a hall into another room, a little further down. At least we got something a little interesting before heading to bed.

A ceiling fan dying in the heat

Flakes of paint looks like underwater image

The night went well with nothing out of the ordinary. We had the whole day to relax and wait for night two. It was 105 degrees and we stayed in the room all day and watched movies and played some board games. We went over audio from the night before and captured all the sounds of the paint chips falling to the floor. I captured a man saying his name was Mike. We captured a couple more EVPs, but nothing that was making this place live up to the name "most haunted". Maybe we just had a bad night and all hell would unleash tonight.

Just prior to dark, I brought out a cake for Daphne since this was her last investigation with the team. Daphne was moving to Colorado. It was dark now, and I had the girls head out and investigate on their own to see if anything would respond to them. They investigated for an hour and came back. They said they heard the same thing, paint falling in the rooms and hallway. The cameras picked up nothing out of the ordinary and the fog went away in the basement. I really wanted to go down there, but no one else wanted to. I went down to check on the camera which was okay. I wrote our names on a door going into the kitchen where others had as well. The night was very quiet and no further activity was recorded. We woke up the next morning and took some final pictures before leaving. My first impression of the manor was, with some clean-up there could be more paranormal findings and less paint chip noise. Maybe another investigation would be in the future.

Kerri, Jay, Radio, Craig, Daphne, Jeremy, and Greg (2013)

## Edinburgh Manor Revisited (2017)

We wanted to go back to the manor again. It has been four years, so I figured all the issues with the paint and mold would be taken care of by now. This time we had some new members with us and one that was here before. We arrived and got all the paperwork out of the way. The first thing I did was head downstairs to check on the mold. It was taken care of, but not in the way it should have been. It was still there, just hidden behind some paneling that covered up the black mold. I guess that was better, but the spores still have a way to release into the air even when covered by something. I told the team we would need masks down there and they told me we would need masks upstairs as well. They showed me all the paint chips everywhere. It was worse now than four years ago, and it smelled very stale. I thought by this time they would have done something to make it more enjoyable. This place could be so much more if taken care of and even the ghosts might like it better. I was glad we only had one night here.

The night came and Jason and I headed to the basement with masks on to ask questions. We heard some loud noises come from down one of the halls between the laundry and the kitchen. There was this creepy feeling that something was in the hall watching us. We heard a louder crash come from the kitchen and headed over to check it out. We were unable to find what made the noises. We headed back down to sit again. I thought I heard a faint scream, but nothing showed up on the recorder. We went to the far hall and down into the boiler-room. It was quiet and no noises were heard and no voices were captured on the recorder. The rest of the team found us in the basement, and Jason and I sat on one side, while Jodi, Tia, and the others sat on the far side. Nothing more was heard in the basement.

We all headed back upstairs to set up basecamp in the same room as last time. We tried investigating in the rooms but again the paint chips were more than I could handle. I spent most of the night watching the cameras while the others investigated. While some of the members on the team had some personal experiences, this was still not enough evidence to say most haunted. I would have spent more time investigating if the building was in better shape. I saw what I saw four years ago and it was over for me. While sleeping that night, I thought I heard something come into the room and then walk out, but that was all I had heard. I captured no further EVPs from our night here. Like always we took a team picture before leaving.

Tia, Katie, Miranda, Jodi, Craig, Trina, and Jason

# CHAPTER 5

# MANSFIELD PRISON MANSFIELD, OHIO

I got a call from some friends of mine that had a paranormal team and they had spots open for Mansfield Prison in Ohio in 2014 and were unable to go. They asked me if I was interested in taking the open spots because they would not be able to get a refund. I said sure, although I needed like fifteen people in all, so that meant I needed to post on our Facebook page for extra people to join us. It didn't take long for people to respond. It was still six months away, but we had time to prepare for the trip and find a hotel in the area that we could put five people in each room.

The cost to investigate ranges from $1,200 to $2,400 depending on the night you want. Ours was on an off night, so it was cheaper to investigate. I found a hotel close by that had a pool that almost took me out of the investigation that will be disclosed a little further down.

## The history of Mansfield Prison

The Ohio State Reformatory, also known as the Mansfield Reformatory, is a historic prison located in Mansfield, Ohio in the United States. It was built between 1886 and 1910 and remained in operation until 1990, when a United States Federal Court ruling ordered the facility to be closed. While this facility was used in a number of films (including several while the facility was still in operation), The film, *The Shawshank Redemption* (1994), was used for the majority of the movie. You will also see footage from the prison in the movie, *Air Force One* with Harrison Ford. A bunch of music videos have also been filmed in the prison by artists like Lil Wayne, Godsmack, and many more.

The history of the Ohio State Reformatory started in 1861; the field where the reformatory would be built was used as a training camp for Civil War soldiers. The camp's name had significant meaning to Ohio as it was named Camp Mordecai Bartley in honor of the Mansfield man who served as Ohio governor in the 1840s.

In 1867, Mansfield was promoted for the placement of the new Intermediate Penitentiary (the original name before it was changed to Ohio State Reformatory). The city raised $10,000 to purchase 30 acres of land for the prison. The cost of the facility was $1,326,769. The Intermediate (Ohio State Reformatory) was intended as just that, a halfway point between the Boys Industrial School in Lancaster and the State Penitentiary in Columbus which was intended to house young first-time offenders. Construction started in 1886 and remained under construction until 1910 due to funding problems which caused construction delays. The original architect for the design was Levi T. Scofield from Cleveland, who used three architectural styles; Victorian Gothic, Richardsonian Romanesque, and Queen Anne. Scofield designed the reformatory with these unique styles to help encourage inmates to become reborn back into their spiritual lives. In 1891, the name was changed from Intermediate Penitentiary to Ohio State Reformatory.

On September 15, 1896, the reformatory opened its doors to its first 150 offenders. These prisoners were brought by train from Columbus and put immediately to work on the prison sewer system and the 25-foot stone wall surrounding the complex. The exterior of the building, which is built from brick and concrete, is designed in the Romanesque style giving the frontage a castle-like appearance.

The Reformatory remained in full operation until December 1990 when it was closed by federal court order, as the result of a prisoners' class action suit citing overcrowding and inhumane conditions. They ordered it be closed by December 1986. This order was known as the Boyd Consent Decree. The closing date was moved to 1990 due to delays in constructing the replacement facility, which stands to the west of the old prison, the Mansfield Correctional Institution.

Most of the grounds and support buildings, including the outer wall, have been demolished since the closing. In 1995, the Mansfield Reformatory Preservation Society was formed. They have turned the prison into a museum and conduct tours to help fund grounds rehabilitation projects and currently work to stabilize the buildings against further deterioration.

The East Cell Block remains the largest freestanding steel cell block in the world at six tiers high. Six hundred singular cells that were arranged six floors high. From 1935 until 1959, Arthur Lewis Glattke was the superintendent. Glattke was respected by professionals and inmates alike. He implemented many reforms such as piped in radio music in the cell blocks. Glattke's wife, Helen Bauer Glattke, died of pneumonia three days following an accident in November 1950, where a handgun discharged when she was reaching into a jewelry box in the family's quarters. Glattke died following a heart attack suffered in his office on February 10, 1959. Over 200 people died at the prison, including two guards who were killed during escape attempts.

The penalties were directed with old-fashioned torture devices comprised of "the butterfly," a method of electro-torture, water tubes, a sweatbox for

Caucasian inmates, and "The Hole" which was a barren, small, and solitary quarantine cell. Along with the likelihood of being tortured, the convicts were also endangered to the extreme by other convicts, horrendous food, rat plague, and transmittable diseases. Special treatment was likely, but only to the prisoners who could find the money to pay for it.

When the Reformatory shut down, gossip started flowing that the prison was haunted by inmates whose spirits were imprisoned forever behind the jail bars. Some of the deceased prison guards who perpetrated torture on the prisoners have also been seen and overheard inside the reformatory. In response, the MRPS features "ghost hunts" and trips. Mansfield is now a recognized site for serious paranormal investigations.

### Getting there is half the fun

We had some really good investigators driving a long distance. Rick, Sheila, Julia, and Jason were in one car. Don and Lauralye headed down from the Sheboygan area. I had Rene, whom I wrote about in my first book and sadly this would be her last investigation with us. I also had Bobby and Jane with me. We followed each other down, although Rick thought I was in the right lane and accidentally turned off into downtown Chicago around 10 p.m. I called him and asked what he was doing. He said to keep going and he would find his way back on the tollway. We headed down the highway and it was about an hour later that Rick called and said the two girls needed a bathroom break and asked if Gary, Indiana was a good place to stop. I did tell him that it is the highest crime rate across the nation. I found out later they stopped at this gas station in the middle of Gary and everybody was looking at them. (He should have told them he was headed to prison to do time.)

I had worked the day before, and I guess Sheila was up for a total of 24 hours when we arrived. Someone had the bright idea that we should go tour the prison and walk around, so we could see it during the day. We all piled into two cars. Some of our investigators that were invited off FB were not getting to town till later in the evening, so it was just us headed off to the prison to check it out. When we drove up from a distance, one could only notice how massive this place was just from the outside. Rick was missing again and drove into the new prison and was taking pictures of that one instead. The police showed up and told them they were not allowed to take pictures of the new prison and he had the wrong one. They were nice about it and pointed out the road to the haunted one. We all headed inside and met with one of the tour coordinators. They were close to closing the tours, so they told us to feel free to walk around since we were doing the investigation that night. The main entrance has most of the offices where the wardens would do their paperwork. There was a gift shop to buy shirts with pictures of the prison on it. The staff told us not to lock ourselves in any of the jail cells because someone with a torch would have to come and get us out. Once locked in there, you would have to wait for help. While walking around on the tour, a girl from another group locked herself in one and was now waiting for help. Moving on from the offices, we were met with this staircase that would take you up to the upper level of cells, and then you had a choice to take a metal spiral staircase up to the next level and so on. You could also walk down the entire length of cells. It was a long way down to the other side, and walking past all these cells kind of creeped me out even though it was daytime. The thought of a crazy prisoner grabbing me as I walked past his cell, entered my mind.

The long walk past the cells

We were told some of the stories about what happened to the prisoners on this cell block. The cell block alone could house about 1500 inmates and was six tiers high. We were told that in the cold winter months some of the inmates on the sixth tier closest to the ceiling would freeze to death and in the summer would have heat stroke. We were also told about solitary confinement for when you were really bad. The allowed time in confinement was around 5 hours, but reports of inmates being in there for more than 30 days were listed. When they brought the food to the inmates in confinement, they would mess with the schedule like serving breakfast at noon, lunch at 7 p.m., and dinner even later. The reason they did that was so the inmates couldn't tell time. There was also no windows or light in confinement, so in time the inmates would lose their minds. Rumor has it that in the basement under all the cells are remains of some that were buried down there. We were looking forward to going down there to check it out.

We continued on with the tour and ran into the library, shower-room, and confessional in the building. These rooms alone were so massive we had to sit back and take it all in. There was a room that was surrounded on all sides like a command center which was used to monitor all the prisoners. We also got to take a peek behind the wall of the cells. It was called the Alley where all the piping and electrical runs. It was really amazing to think if you tried to tunnel your way through the wall, you would end up in this corridor that goes all the way down. I don't recall if anyone tried to escape this way at all. Some of our team now was checking out the cells and walking in and out of them to have their pictures taken. We were careful not to close the door behind us, or we would be doing some time inside. Julia was playing it safe and standing in the doorway to one of the cells.

Jason and Craig standing by cell block

It was time to go grab some food and head back to the hotel to get some rest before the big investigation. I decided it was a great idea to take a quick swim in the pool before sleeping. Everyone else followed my lead and came down to the pool area. I had this great idea to try to race Sheila and Julia across the pool saying, "I can beat you guys." Guess what? I won but not before tweaking my hamstring in the pool making it almost impossible to stand on my right leg without support. Sheila stubbed her toe on the side of the pool and was trying to walk off the pain. I limped back up to the room and was chatting with Don. I said, "I don't know if I am going to be able to stand tonight on the investigation." I decided to take a nap and see if it would get better before we leave. I woke up around 6 p.m. and got up and my leg was fine. I was happy that I was going to be able to investigate.

## The Investigation of Mansfield Prison

Our team arrived at the prison along with about six other guests that came with us. We needed fifteen people to come to Mansfield, so we had others with us that follow our Facebook page. We were led inside to the offices of the original prison to get the waivers out of the way. There was a gift shop with shirts that you could buy to let everyone know you were there. After signing the waivers, the host gave us a tour, although most of us knew where to go since we spent the day before wandering around in there. I tell you, when the lights are turned off, it's a whole new place. We separated into three different groups since we had so many people and headed to certain sections of the prison.

I had Rick, Sheila, and Julia with me and we worked the main area of the cells down the corridors. We had the two girls sit in the jail cells on the old beds. The paint in all the cells was flaking off with chips all over the floor. There was a toilet in the room with rust in the bottom, a reminder that at one time these were functioning toilets where hardened criminals did their business. Rick sat down on one and made a face. There was a mirror in the cell, but it wasn't made out of glass. It was made out of stainless steel so the inmate wouldn't be able to take the glass out and cut someone. We decided to leave the two girls in there alone, and Rick and I walked down to the end of the cells. When we tried to shine our flashlight back to the other side, the distance was so great that we were unable to see the other side. We listened quietly, and I swear I heard a whisper come from behind me in one of the cells. Not long after that we heard some screams coming from the girls, so we rushed over to see what was up. They said while they were sitting on the bed something sat down next to them. They felt the pressure on the springs. That made all the hair stand up on our necks. I mean whatever was there, it could see us and we can't see them, and it's a heck of a long jog to the other side to get away if something took chase.

Julia and Sheila in the spot where the ghost sat

Don and Lauralye and some others were investigating down in the detention block. This was the place where the inmates would get locked in for long periods of time. This was also where one poor tour guest accidently locked herself in while we were there. She had to wait for a locksmith to get her out. Don and the group set up a stand-alone DVR system run off batteries in that area to see if they could capture anything. They told us they heard footsteps and noises coming from within the cells there. Later in the night, on review of the video feed, Don found out someone tripped over the DVR cord unplugging it from the battery, so anything they would have caught on camera was null and void. Our group headed down below the cells to the basement where it is rumored that people are buried. I had asked why they don't look for the bodies and was told that if they find one then they have to do this long investigation process so they don't look for what they think is there. I am not sure on the truth to that concept. When we went down there it was hard to stand in some spots as the floor was right above us. The floor of the basement had sand piles that were raised up in some spots and flat in others. There were some cement slabs that looked like it was once a cement floor, but then stopped and the sand started again. There were tons of pipes and duct work down there heading off in all directions. When we turned off the lights it felt like we were in lockdown. I couldn't see my hand in front of my face. Rick thought something touched him on his shoulder and Sheila heard a whispered voice behind her. I felt a cobweb on my face. It is sometimes said that the feeling of cobwebs are the spirits touching you, although being that this was the basement, it very well could be cobwebs. I turned on the light and didn't see any webs at all. We sat there for quite a while with some noises of feet rubbing on cement close to us, but on inspection found nothing that we could see. We started hearing really loud banging, a floor or so above us, we thought. We headed up to see where it was coming from. One of the other investigators decided to make believe he was a corrections officer and had a nightstick and was going from cell to cell banging on it. He was telling the inmates to get back in their cells or they would be going to solitary confinement. I am not sure if that was working, but I know that some of the investigators were unaware that he was going to do this, which halted the rest of the investigations, since no one could hear anything. The host had brought in pizza for us, which was a good time to eat and let the one investigator play the officer.

Round two of the investigations sent Lauralye and Don to the chapel area of the prison. Bobby and Jane along with the fake prison guard headed off to some upstairs rooms that consisted of an attic and nurses, station, where the prisoners would have gone if sick or hurt. Rick, Sheila, Julia, and I met up with Jason in the shower room, where he was doing some 360-degree shots. We stayed there for a while and kept hearing footsteps and other odd noises like breathing or grunts. Nothing was found in this area that could have caused that. We headed upstairs to see if we could find Bobby and Jane, but they seemed to have vanished. We stayed in the nursing area and heard what sounded like a wheelchair moving down the hallway. We peeked around the corner and saw a wheelchair. No one could tell me if it was in that spot when we walked in the room or not. We marked it with tape to see if it would move. I didn't find out till the car ride home that Bobby and Jane that had vanished really did so. They hopped up on a ladder and ventured down behind a wall which was the out-of-bounds area where no one was supposed to go. They said they saw a spot that looked like it was off the map and wanted to peek inside. They found a small little antique pouch of smoking tobacco which we think no one else found before as well. Well it was a little late to yell and say that they shouldn't have done that.

Lauralye and Don were in the chapel sitting in the dark asking questions about what they learned in the chapel, when suddenly Lauralye saw a large ball of white light floating inside the room and pointed it out to Don. It stayed in the room for a bit, then floated past a open door and vanished. Lauralye asked the host about the ball of light she had seen and he said that other guest and investigators had seen this light as well in that area.

We had only 3 hours left to investigate, and I had this massive headache coming on, likely from lack of sleep the night before. I said I would bug out early and head back to the hotel. The rest of the team would finish the investigation and let me know if anything more happened.

Rick told me that he and Julia were using K2 meters in the detention block and they were both lighting up for a while to the questions they were asking. The rest of the team said it was quiet for the most part. This was one of the few investigations where we only had one night to investigate. It was a really neat investigation since two movies were made here and the history alone was worth going. I would like to go back again in the future and check it out one more time and I am sure Don feels the same way seeing he lost the video feed that night.

Taking a peek with the thermal camera

# CHAPTER 6

# PROSPECT PLACE
# TRINWAY, OHIO

The team at Prospect Place

I **saw this place** on a listing for haunted places and thought it would be an interesting investigation. It is known for being part of the underground railway to help slaves get to freedom. There was a very interesting history to the place, so we decided to call them and set up a two-night investigation there.

## The History of Prospect Place

Prospect Place, also known as Trinway Mansion was a 29-room mansion built by abolitionist George Willison Adams in 1856. Today, it is the home of the non-profit G. W. Adams Educational Center, Inc. The mansion is listed on the National Register of Historic Places and the Ohio Underground Railroad Association's list of Underground Railroad sites.

This home featured many new and, for the time, revolutionary innovations. It had indoor plumbing which included a copper tank on the second floor which pressurized water throughout the house. Two coal stoves had copper tanks which heated water and allowed the home to have both hot and cold running water service.

This is the second house to stand on the same foundation. The first house was destroyed by an arson-related fire shortly after its completion. The mansion was rebuilt after the fire, with modern fire stopping added to it. The interior walls of the current house are solid brick, and there is a 2-inch layer of mortar between the first and second floors of the house to block fire.

Prospect Place also featured a unique refrigeration system to cool milk, cheese, butter, etc. A primitive form of "air conditioning" was created by bringing cool basement air into the living quarters during the summer months via ducts in the outside walls.

The Underground Railroad operation conducted by G. W. Adams and his brother, Edward, was a huge undertaking. The brothers operated a flouring mill on the Ohio and Erie Canal and owned warehouses, a boat yard, and cooper shops in Dresden, Ohio. When men from the Adams' company would take flour to New Orleans, Louisiana, they would return with refugees (runaway slaves) beneath the decks of their boats.

The mansion passed through the Adams-Cox family to George Cox, a grandson of G. W. Adams, who owned the property until the 1960s. In 1969 the home was sold to a distant relative of George Cox, Eugene Cox. Eugene operated a gravel mining company, the Cox Gravel Company, which proceeded to mine the remaining 275 acres (1.1 km$^2$) associated with the estate.

While the Cox Gravel Company owned the Prospect Place mansion, it was listed on the National Register of Historic Places. The deterioration of the mansion increased due to lack of maintenance and vandalism. The interior of the building was all but gutted by thieves and vandals. The estate was scheduled to be demolished in 1988. Local businessman Dave Longaberger purchased the house to prevent its destruction.

Dave Longaberger installed a new roof on the structure and increased security with the intention of restoring the home as a future Longaberger Company headquarters building. Upon choosing to construct the current headquarters of the Longaberger Basket Company in Newark, Ohio, he placed the mansion restoration project on hold.

Dave Longaberger died of cancer in the 1990s. The Longaberger Company continued to maintain security on the property until 2001, when the great-great-grandson of G. W. Adams and Longaberger relative, George J. Adams, purchased the home with the goal of finishing the restoration.

George J. Adams had investors for the project, to include adaptive reuse with a restaurant in the building. After the September 11, 2001 attacks, the investors backed out.

Adams created a non-profit, the G. W. Adams Education Center, Inc., which has owned the building since 2005. The educational center has continued the restoration.

The building was featured in an episode of Ghost Hunters on the SyFy Channel in April 2008. It was also featured on *Ghost Adventures* on the Travel Channel on January 1, 2010.

### The rumors of the haunting

The following are stories of the ghosts who haunt Prospect Place. Many visitors who have come to the house, claim to have had paranormal encounters here, and these experiences are based on sights and sounds that include voices in empty rooms, the laughter of a child, hair-raising whispers, shadowy apparitions, and even the ghost of a man in formal attire who has been seen standing near the main staircase on an upper floor. The ghost of George W. Adams himself is said to haunt the place. Some stories say that he loved the place so much that his spirit simply refuses to leave it.

Most feel that the ghosts who linger here are those of slaves who sought refuge here during the period when it was a station on the Underground Railroad. There have been reported sightings here of a black woman. She is often seen in the basement rooms.

There is also another story that might explain the hauntings in the basement, especially those reports of cold chills being felt and the anguished cries that have sometimes been heard. There was a train wreck that occurred near Dresden on a hot summer day in the late 1800s. A passenger train had been stopped on the tracks because of a problem with the locomotive and another train came along and collided with it from behind. The engine of the second trail barreled into the passenger cars and its boiler exploded. Many of the passengers died instantly, while others were badly burned. There was no hospital nearby. As it happened, Prospect Place was the closest house to the accident site and so the cool basement of the house was turned into a temporary hospital for the injured passengers. A number of them succumbed to their wounds while waiting for assistance, however, and it is said that many of their ghosts still haunt the dark basement rooms.

The most widely known story about the house in the area involving ghosts tells of a young girl who died after falling from a porch on the house during one harsh winter the 1860s. Her body could not be buried because the ground was too frozen to dig her grave, so her body was kept on ice in the basement of the house until spring. She was the daughter of a local family and so her mother came each day to visit her until her corpse was finally laid to rest.

Since that time, guests have often reported seeing her ghost in the hallways and especially around one of the fireplaces. Childish laughter has also been heard in the house, as well as the sobs of the grieving mother.

## The investigation

We arrived at Prospect Place and had two nights to investigate. We picked two of the big rooms there to stay in overnight. It was warm out with no AC, but we brought some fans along to put in the windows to blow some cooler air in. We walked around the rooms to get a feel for the place. There was a steep staircase going up to the second level. There was a smaller one going to the very top of what you would call a lookout, although when we got up there we saw lots of bird droppings all over the place. It was covered to the point where the floor was white, and I am not a big fan of bird poop since birds carry diseases. I wasn't going to be spending much time up here. The basement which housed the tunnels from when it was an underground railroad was only accessible from outside. We headed down there and saw a couple different rooms in the basement area. The underground tunnels were buried now, but you could tell where they used to be. There was a barn on the property that is said to be haunted by a person that was after the slaves. The rumor is they caught him on the property and hung him in the barn. I saw on previous investigations that teams were getting some evidence on the second floor of the barn. We noticed it was now blocked off to the second floor, so we would have to investigate from down below. The mosquitoes during the day were bad and I had a feeling they would be worse at night. We all went inside to set up some cameras and then relax till it was dark and time to investigate.

We started the investigation by sending a group upstairs. Rick, Jason, Julia, and I went down to the basement to see what we could capture. We each took a room in the basement and I had my back to the darkness. While I was asking some questions in the basement, something touched my arm and pulled on my shirt. Could this have been the girl that was left down here all winter till the ground warmed up enough for them to bury her? I sat there a little longer and asked some more questions and heard a whisper of someone right behind me, and it sounded like a girl's voice. I played back my voice recorder and we heard a girl's voice say, "Help me." The hair stood up on all of our necks. We went back to our spots to see if anything else would happen. Julia thought she felt something touch her hair and caress it. I got that spiderweb feeling on my face which sometimes is associated with a spirit touching you. Rick heard some footsteps come up behind him and then stop. Nothing happened after that and it seemed calmer in the basement. We headed upstairs to see if anything was going on with the rest of the team.

We met with Terrance and the rest of the team. He stated that Maggie was in one of the rooms and felt very sad as if something bad had happened in there. She is sensitive and sometimes could sense things around her. Other than that occurrence nothing else happened. We switched to the upstairs while the rest went downstairs. We went to the room on the second floor which now had a picture of a cross on it. It was painted on there over what they said was some drawings of devil signs, where they used to worship some dangerous things. It was also said that this area had some bad energy in it. We again sat there in silence, first to see if anything moved or made some noise. Nothing happened, so we asked if anything was there and if they could make a noise. We heard something moving on the floor above which was the lookout tower. We ventured up above to see if we could find it. The noise was coming from the birds that were residing in the tower. We made a note of that for future trips to this area.

The cross that was painted over the bad symbols

We met up with the team that was in the basement and they reported some more footsteps but were not touched by anything like we were. We all decided to head out to the barn to see if we could get any acitivty out there at all. We got tons of bug bites but captured no activity. We gathered no further evidence that night so headed off to sleep.

We slept really good with nothing out of the ordinary to report while sleeping. We headed out during the day to check out the local surroundings and came across Route 666, so we ended up taking a few pictures by the sign. We headed back and hung out most of the day taking some 360-degree pictures with the place in the backdrop. We decided to try something a little different tonight, so we sent Julia upstairs by herself in one of the rooms that is supposed to have some activity. She was not up there more than an hour; when she came down she looked white as a ghost. Something had startled her in the room and she felt like it was attached to her. She said she didn't feel quite right and was not feeling good at all. We had her take a break for a while in the cool bedroom to see if she would feel better. Jason didn't like the idea of some ghost picking on Julia, so he headed up there to have some words with the ghost. We don't provoke ghosts at all; however, if something is messing with our investigators, we might angrily ask them why they were doing that and it's not right. That kind of tone may make them mad, but then maybe they will tell us why. We don't call them names nor do we make fun of them. Jason came back down and said he heard some loud knocks come from the room Julia was in, but nothing else. It was a very slow night other than Julia getting worked up by something. We heard some noises in the basement and some shuffling of feet down there one last time. I jumped a little bit while sitting next to the hole that was the tunnel. Something grabbed my leg while I was sitting there and startled me. My mind wandered in thinking something came up out of the hole and wanted to bring me down there. We attempted to investigate the barn again, but nothing was heard. Julia was feeling better and back to herself.

The next morning we headed home. I called Terrance who was driving with the rest of the team and asked where they were on the road. I found out they were behind us. He told me they had to go back to do a cleansing at the house because of Jason yelling at the ghost. I said, "What are you talking about?" He said, Jason made an presence angery, and while they were sleeping in the other bedroom, something was kicking the air mattress that Terrance was sleeping on. Maggie woke up and saw his air mattress was flopping up in the air and his arms were swinging all over the place while he was asleep. I found it odd that they never said anything to us. I returned home to go over the video. I reviewed the night that Terrance and Maggie slept in the room. At no time was the mattress moving in the room. Terrance's arms never left his side except to roll over and Maggie never woke up.

# CHAPTER 7

# WAVERLY HILLS SANATORIUM LOUISVILLE, KENTUCKY

The investigators at Waverly Hills

**W**averly Hills a place on everyone's bucket list. It is next to impossible to book a night in this place because it's sold out in less than 24 hours. We were lucky enough to have a couple people booking on the day that the dates were released, and I managed to find a day that worked. We needed fifteen or more people to go to keep the price down, so we invited some extra friends of ours to come along. This is listed as one of the scariest places on earth.

## The History

During the 1800s and early 1900s, America was ravaged by a deadly disease known by many as the, "white death" or better known as tuberculosis. This terrifying and very contagious plague, for which no cure existed, claimed entire families and sometimes entire towns. In 1900, Louisville, Kentucky had one of the highest tuberculosis death rates. In 1910, a hospital was constructed in Jefferson County that had been designed to combat the horrific disease. The hospital quickly became overcrowded and with donations of money and land, a new hospital was started in 1924.

Waverly Hills, opened two years later in 1926. It was considered the most advanced tuberculosis sanatorium in the country, but even then, most of the patients succumbed to the disease. It was thought that the best treatment for tuberculosis was fresh air and lots of rest. Many patients survived their stay at Waverly Hills, but it is estimated that hundreds died here at the height of the epidemic.

In many cases, the treatments for the disease were as bad as the disease itself. Some of the experiments that they did in search of a cure seem barbaric by today's standards, but others are now common practice. Patient's lungs were exposed to ultraviolet light to try and stop the spread of bacteria. This was done in "sun rooms", using artificial light in place of sunlight, or on the roof or open porches of the hospital. Since fresh air was thought to also be a possible cure, patients were often placed in front of huge windows or on the open porches, no matter what the season. Old photographs show patients lounging in chairs, taking in the fresh air, while literally covered with snow.

Some treatments were less pleasant, and much bloodier. Balloons were surgically implanted in the lungs and then filled with air to expand them. This often had disastrous results, and operations where muscles and ribs were removed from a patient's chest to allow the lungs to expand further and let in more oxygen. This blood-soaked procedure was a "last resort" and few of the patients survived it.

Patients that survived both the disease and the treatments left Waverly Hills, but most patients left through what is called the Body Chute. This enclosed tunnel for the dead led from the hospital to the railroad tracks at the bottom of the hill. A motorized rail and cable system moved the bodies and were lowered in secret to the waiting trains. This was done so that patients would not see how many were leaving the hospital as corpses.

In 1961, Waverly Hills was closed but was reopened a year later as Woodhaven Geriatrics Sanatorium. There have been many rumors and stories told about patient mistreatment and unusual experiments during the years that the building was used as old-age home. Electroshock therapy, which was highly effective in those days, was widely used for a variety of ailments. Budget cuts in the 1960s and 1970s led to both horrible conditions and patient mistreatments, and in 1982, the state closed the facility for good.

## Legends of Waverly Hills

When people in a sanatorium died, you'd expect it to be the tuberculosis patients, not the healthy staff. This room 502 seemed to be a center for disaster. According to local legend, in 1928, the head nurse of 502 was found hanging from a light fixture. This was believed to be a suicide, triggered by depression over an unwanted pregnancy.

Four years later, another nurse who worked in room 502 jumped off the roof patio to her death. While no records exist to explain why she did this, some believe she was pushed off the edge.

One of the saddest ghost stories is that of an elderly woman who supposedly roams the hospital, moaning and bleeding from her chained hands and feet. If you approach her, she runs away.

One of the more well-known ghosts at Waverly Hills is a little boy known as Timmy. He was around six or seven years old when he died in the hospital. Since he died with his whole life ahead of him, his spirit wanders the hospital trying to have fun. Visitors often bring balls for him to play with, and many claim they see the balls moving, seemingly on their own.

The Creeper is a dark, terrifying entity that crawls along the floors and the walls of Waverly Hills. Some believe it's an otherworldly spirit or a demonic force, while others believe it's a human spirit that's been twisted by the trauma of tubercular death. Some have even said if you see him your life changes forever.

Doppelgängers also known as "double-walkers" are a type of spirit that can mimic the appearance, voice, and mannerisms of anyone or anything it encounters. This could mean looking across the room and seeing an exact replica of yourself.

Tour guides at Waverly Hills reported seeing doppelgängers of themselves and others. In some cases, the doppelgängers were almost identical, except for black holes where the eyes should be.

### The Investigation

We left the hotel during a wicked rain storm, so we took our time driving to Waverly Hills. We found a small road leading up to the place and found a big fence with some cameras pointing at us. I called and said we were out by the gate. A few minutes later a guy showed up with a golf cart to open the fence so we could drive through. We went past a wooded area and through the trees was a massive building with lots of windows. The floors above the windows were open. We spent some time walking around the building before coming back in with the owner. I had asked the owner if animals could get inside. He said that the only thing that was in there were bats and birds. I heard from another team about 10 years ago there were some raccoons in there. The owner said that was when the tree branches reached the roof, but all those were cut away and he confirmed again that only bats and birds can get to the second floor. He has security cameras on all the floors so he knows what gets into the building and what doesn't. He said they have had lots of problems with kids trying to break in. I saw a video a month before where some kids were on video tossing bricks through the windows, and of course, they were caught on camera and by the police.

We all headed inside to sign some waivers and visit the gift shop. There was a bunch of tables and chairs in the room. This was going to be our set up area for all of our equipment and to figure out what groups of us would be together. I decided that we were not going to set up the DVR and cameras this time. The size of the building was so great that the 100 feet of cable was not going to hardly reach anywhere. We only had one night in here and I wasn't going to waste an hour setting up cameras. I told my team to use their hand-held cameras instead. We were splitting up into two teams with Rick, Kerri, and Jay leading one group and Sheila, Jennifer, Julia, and I leading the rest of the team. There are five floors here and a roof area that we had access to.

I said I was going to visit the Bodychute and check that place out first and the other team would head to the upper floors. Someone told me the Body Chute is so long that it resides in two different area codes. I am not sure if that is correct or not. We got to the top of the chute and Sheila shined her flashlight down into the darkness. I had a brighter flashlight and smaller beam of light and was able to see the gate at the far end of the chute. We all said we were going to walk down to the very end before we leave. I walked down about 30 stairs and stopped. Julia and Jennifer sat near the top of the chute to try to record with the camera that had night vison on it. Sheila was brave enough and walked down almost to the end of the tunnel. We all turned off our flash-lights and it was pitch black. We were sitting in a tunnel that is famous yet so disturbing to think about. The tunnel that brought hundreds of the dead that passed away down to the train at the bottom, where they would be taken away to mass graves. We have never investigated anywhere with this much tragedy.

I asked questions while using the Ghost-Box to see if someone died and was taken away in the chute. Voices came back and said "Yes," and right after this voice came through, there was this sudden cold breeze that shot through the tunnel. It turned off the ghost box, and Sheila was saying, "Oh God," but I don't think God was there at that moment. There was a loud noise close to the end of the tunnel. I didn't have to ask Sheila if she heard it, as she was on her way back up to us. We now sat close to each other. Julia thought some-thing had touched her on the shoulder and I felt something brush my leg and another breeze went past me. I shined my light down into the tunnel and we all thought we saw a shadow cross in front of my light. This was something that was reported here by other teams. There were some other odd noises, but it did rain before we got here, and I could hear some water landing on some-thing metal. There were other noises that we could not explain. Jennifer's video camera was also acting up and not wanting to record properly which also happens quite a bit at Waverly Hills. We also thought we heard footsteps coming from down below, but they were drowned out by the airplane going over. I heard a few train whistles from outside as well. I said we might have a problem recording with all the planes and trains.

We decided to switch with the other team and headed back to the base area. I heard the rest of the team heading down the stairs toward us. Kerri told me that some of the team were walking really slow, so they walked up to the roof for a little while to see what it was like. Kerri said she heard something run out onto the roof, and whatever it was pulled down the back of her shirt. Jay was standing behind her and saw her shirt get grabbed by something. The roof is known for ghosts of children that like to play sometimes with balls, although in this moment Kerri's shirt would have to do. The rest in the group caught up to them but said they heard nothing other than planes. I told them I heard that inside the body chute as well.

The Body Chute

We all took a quick break and pizza was brought in for something to eat before heading back out into the massive darkness. I ran into Jodi who was on her way in from outside. She said up on the fifth floor she saw a shadow in the hallway. We were headed that way to see what we could see. The hallways go on forever in this place and stop at a corner and then continue on down further to the very end. I wanted to see room 502 since that was where the suicides occurred. I sat in there for a while with nothing happening. We heard some noises out in the hall area and walked back out. There were lots of water on the floor, so if anything was walking on the floors, you would see the footprints, but the only ones there were ours. I decided to split our team up in the hall and the rooms. I put Julia and Jennifer down at the very end of the hall. I had Sheila sit next to me. I had Lisa sit in 502 to see if anything would happen while we were in the hall. It was quite breezy up there since there are no windows on the upper floors. The lack of windows was so the patients could sit in the open air which they thought was good for their lungs. I started out having Julia use the box on the other end of the hallway and ask questions. She asked what floor they were on and how long they were here. A voice came back and said floor 2 and that they were here for six years. It is amazing when you get an intelligent response to questions that you ask. I had my voice recorder on as well, however, you could only record for about 7 minutes at a time. You then had to wait for the airplane to go over and the thunderous noise from the jet engines to stop. Then another one comes. I was thinking how in the world do other teams investigate here and get such good results and EVPs. I was only getting 7 minutes at a time and the planes were all making us mad. We paid quite a bit of money to investigate this place and everyone was disappointed with all the noise pollution. The only place that you could hear more of the knocks and bangs was in the chute where the planes were muffled quite a bit more. We figured that we would take some pictures in the rooms and I would take pictures down the hall. I told Sheila to turn the other way so my flash would not blind her. I took about fifteen photos in all directions of the halls hoping to capture something. I would have to go over the photos later on when I get back to motel. We decided to head down to the breakroom and see how the other team did in the basement and the chute.

Rick and Radio said it was extremely quiet in the chute and nothing was happening. Some were tired from the long walk to the bottom and back up. I said I wanted to try the chute one more time and then upstairs one more time as well. So we went to the chute and Rick and others went upstairs. Well, Rick was right, nothing was going on in the chute at all. It almost felt like nothing was there this time or maybe moved to a different part of the building. We were only there a half hour and were getting nothing, so we headed to the break room to get some more pizza and wait for Rick and the rest of them.

Rick came back with Lauralye who was on one of the upper floors and it was a muggy night just after the rain. She said she felt a cold breeze come from the left of her and the K2 meter was going off right around where she was standing. It stayed cold for a bit, then went away, and the K2 stopped as well. We wondered who she ran into up there. Maybe it was the nurse that committed suicide in 502.

Time sure flies when you are having fun. I wanted to go one last time upstairs to see if we could hear some more noises. I saw on one of the corners out from the hallway this time and the women sat in different sections of the hallway to see what they might hear. It was an oddly quiet last part of the investigation. I could hear nothing other than some birds waking up in the early morning hours. We were going to have to get back to the hotel and get some sleep before driving back in the morning. We all headed downstairs. I walked past this one room that was the morgue and saw a body inside on the gurney. I looked again and saw it move, but it was just Jason who thought it would be cool to lie inside. Just before getting to the breakroom, I headed to the chute so that I could walk to the end of it and back before we left. It was easy going down but not so easy coming back up and I was not tired. I met with the other group and they were heading back to the hotel as well. I had lots of video and recordings to go over when I get back. We thanked the owners and we all agreed that this building was very interesting to see, but we were unhappy with all the planes.

Craig sitting in a room next to the hallway

Eyes captured when I was taking pictures in the hall

The eyes that I had captured was in the long hallway of Waverly Hills on the fifth floor. Sheila was next to me looking away from the flash. Julia and Jennifer were down past the eyes on the other side of it. (noted with the arrow in white) We also saw no other tracks in the water on either side other than human footprints. Some say this was the Creeper we captured.

# CHAPTER 8

# WILLIAM A. IRVIN
# DULUTH MINNESOTA

I always wanted to do something different since we always investigate hospitals, schools, and other buildings. I wanted to do the Queen Mary but that was too far away. I found an old iron ore ship that was docked in Duluth, MN.

It had a history of being haunted and also allowed teams to come in and investigate. I called and was able to pick a night that worked for our team.

## The History

*William A. Irvin* is a lake freighter, named after William A. Irvin, that sailed as a bulk freighter on the Great Lakes as part of US Steel's lake fleet. The freighter was a flagship of the company fleet from her launch in the depths of the depression in 1938 until 1975. She was the workhorse of the fleet until her retirement in 1978.

The ship was refurbished and is moored in Duluth, Minnesota, as a museum ship. It is a well-maintained example of a straight decker, as she has no self-unloading system.

The ship was listed on the National Register of Historic Places in 1989 for her state-level significance in the themes of engineering, maritime history, and transportation.

The ship was launched in November 1937, at the American Ship Building Company in Lorain, Ohio. Her maiden voyage was in June 1938. The ship was the first of a four-vessel class, including *Governor Miller, John Hulst,* and *Ralph H. Watson*; each costing about US $1.3 million. After christening by William Irvin's wife, Gertrude Irvin, and sea trials, *William A. Irvin* went to work hauling bulk materials from the tip of Lake Superior down to US Steel's mills on Lakes Michigan and Erie. She and her three sisters incorporated many technological features in their design and proved themselves excellent workers. She also hauled many company guests in the boat's exceptional luxury on behalf of US Steel. She steamed for the Pittsburgh Steamship Division of US Steel for her entire career. On 27 August 1940, the ship set a record by unloading 13,856 tons of ore in 2 hours 55 minutes using Hulett unloaders. This record still stands as of 2018 and is unlikely to be broken, because all ships today use automatic self-unloaders in the bottom of their cargo holds.

The ship sat in layup in West Duluth for 8 years until the Duluth Entertainment Convention Center purchased her for $110,000 for an addition to their convention center along the Duluth waterfront. She was repainted and sealed up before heading to her final dock near the Aerial Lift Bridge where she sits today as a museum ship.

The ship was one of few built with a three-tiered bow cabin, as opposed to the standard two. The extra deck is used to house a suite of four guest cabins and a guest lounge. Also, a part of the guest accommodations was a guest dining room located where the number two hatch would be on most. Those parts of the boat are trimmed in oak paneling and walnut veneer with brass handrailings. The William A. Irvin and her sisters were some of the first to be powered by DeLaval Cross steam turbines as opposed to the standard reciprocating triple expansion steam engines. The ship also included welding in much of her construction and was also the first to have all areas of the ship accessible from the interior of the ship which allowed the boat's crew to stay inside during rough weather.

The only recorded death was a sailor who is said to haunt the ship was Mr. William Wuori. He was the only sailor to have died aboard the ship. They believe many more sailors have come back to haunt the ship as well.

## The Investigation

We only had a few investigators that could make it this time to the investigation. We all piled into one car and headed to Duluth, Minnesota. We got down there a few hours early and they were still giving tours so we ventured around town. It was extremely busy with a marathon in town and they had some bands playing downtown. I asked a bystander at the beer tent how long the band was playing tonight, and he told us about 1 a.m. Seeing that the ship was only a few blocks away, I had a funny feeling we would be hearing music too, which kind of messes up being able to hear voices that are quiet. Well, nothing we could do about it now, but in the future we should check to make sure there are no events going on in town. Duluth is a very interesting place and visiting the harbor with the liftbridge and lighthouse was a bonus.

Jeremy, Craig, Jennifer, Lisa, and Jason in Duluth

We headed back to the ship and met Alex Dunning who would be our host for the night and show us around. We signed a waiver in the guest area with all the souvenirs. Almost every place we go to investigate that is famous, has a gift shop to buy things to show that you visited. Alex was the lead and would give us a tour before we got started. Once you leave the gift shop area, you can go off in many different directions. We headed down to the engine room to check out the furnace area since this was one of the few spots that someone actually died. This whole area was massive and had lots of places you could fall if you were not careful. We headed down to the bottom of the ship. The ladders headed down to the bottom were very steep and narrow. Once down in the bottom, there were tons of haunted props since they hold a haunted boat here in October every year. It's a huge haunt, and Alex said it takes about 45 min to go through the whole thing. It is also a very haunted area of the ship. Doors are said to slam on certain rooms of the haunt, loud bangs and knocks and sometimes disembodied voices can be heard. We were hoping for all of this to happen. We walked the maze just to see it and it was very unique for a haunted boat. We got to the other side of the ship away from some of the props and I looked up to the top of the ship where the ore was poured in. I felt very small inside this ship as I looked up to the top of the hatches that covered the different sections of the ship. We made our way up to the Captains quarters and guest areas where the important guests would sleep. It was very cozy and I would have no problem sleeping in there. They had a shower and toilet in each area and they even had a fireplace. It was time to get down to business and end the tour. I was already tired and out of breath from going up and down the stairs on each side of the ship.

## The Investigation

We started down in the room where the only recorded death had occurred. We had all the lights off. We all stayed together on this investigation since there was only the five of us. We asked questions to see if anyone was down there with us. We all heard some loud knocks come from behind the furnace where coal would have been tossed in to make the ship go faster. I heard what sounded like footsteps above us as well. There was another really loud knock that came from behind the furnaces again. We stepped back there to see if we could see anything and nothing was there. We sat in the darkness for a little while longer and heard some smaller taps, but they seemed to be hitting somewhere. I thought it must be raining outside. I went closer to the noises, and yes a little rain was sneaking inside. The louder knocks and footsteps were not caused by the rain.

We all moved deeper into the ship and down lots of steep stairs again. I knew I would be sore in the morning. We made it down to the bottom of the ship where the haunted house maze was. Alex explained that there would be lots of loud bangs and things moving in this area when no one was there. We found a spot close to one of the props and sat down. It didn't take long for us to hear loud footsteps that my voice recorder was picking up as well. The footsteps sounded like they had walked onto the upper deck and was headed our way. They seemed to have stopped close to a utility room. I asked if it was possible someone got on board. Alex said, "No, that the only way on board now would be to climb the huge rope over the water." It would be next to impossible to do this as it went straight up. Well, whatever just walked across the boat was really close to us now, only one room away. I said "Marko" and "Polo" came back as the response clear as day, and we all heard it. Wow! A disembodied voice that we all heard and whoever it was just got started. I went over some audio and captured just in that section answers to our questions.

Question "Who is there?"
Answer "I am"
Question "What is this place?"
Answer "A boat"

We all moved from that section and headed down further toward the other end of the haunt. We sat next to the walls and just listened in the dark. Again we heard footsteps followed by what sounded like quick bangs. They stopped and then the bangs started again. Jason and Jeremy walked over toward the direction of where the noise was coming from. Debunked would be the conclusion as they found out one of the props air tanks that made the monster move was on. We decided to take a quick break before heading to the captains quarters and the guest quarters.

We got to the captains area and saw his bed where he slept near the front of the ship. On his desk was the maps enclosed in plastic of the depths of the lake. We walked down to the guest area with the individual bedrooms and fireplaces. Each room had a bathroom. It felt really cozy. Jeremy and I hung out in one of the rooms to see if something would communicate with us. It was really quiet in this area. It's possible the ghosts were in bed too. Jennifer and Lisa were sitting in another room when I heard Jennifer say something sat down next to her on the bed. She felt the bed move and she had stayed still. We came over to that area and sure enough the K2 meter went off when we got close to the bed. It lasted for a few seconds and then was gone. We all headed over to the last section of the boat with the mess hall and some offices on the other side of the boat. It was a long walk to the other side and it was raining lightly and the deck was quite slippery. We were walking right past all the deck lids that would normally be removed when filling with iron ore. However, they no longer do this, so they are firmly in place.

We made it over to the other side and ducked inside the mess hall and sat down to have a conversation with the cooks who were no longer there. There was a weird flash of white light in the room and there were no ship out on the water. It was not the lighthouse either, and we were too high for car lights. We were not sure what caused it. I then heard what sounded like singing and it seemed to be getting louder. Too bad it was coming from outside the ship where the band was playing a couple blocks away. We decided we wouldn't be able to hear much in the mess hall and walked back down the hall to the offices on each side and some bedrooms for the cooks. I sat in one of the bedrooms and something next to me moved in the room. I felt as though someone was watching me, someone I could not see. This part of the boat's bedrooms seemed to bother me a little more. It could have been because they were not as nice as the other ones. I felt like there was a few things with us in the rooms. We all started to hear noises coming from some of the rooms. Jason heard something fly onto the floor like a small rock or something, but nothing could be found. We asked some questions and thought we heard some voices, but it ended up being the band again. I really wanted to investigate more in this area but knew it would be hard to hear anything. It was after 1 a.m. now and we were unable to book any rooms this weekend due to the marathon in town, so we had a long drive back to Wisconsin. We thanked Alex and agreed that we all wanted to come back in the future when there is no event going on so close to the ship.

The coal-burning furnace where someone died

# CHAPTER 9

# PAULDING LIGHT
# BRUCE CROSSING, MICHIGAN

The investigation of the Paulding Light

**W**hen I was in high school in the 80s, I would always hear my classmates talking about the light or have you been to the light?

I finally asked what they were talking about and they told me that it's a light that chases your car when you park on a hill. I am not sure if I really believed them. There is much more to this fable than what meets the eye. I know some reading this article are going to argue the fact that it's real. I will go into detail and even offer up a link where we debunked the paulding light and we are not the only ones. There are many groups before us who found the truth to what is really going on and still no one believes in the truth. Some say, well, unsolved mysteries was out there and they can't find the answer to it. Have you looked up the cast to unsolved mysteries? They are actors in a show that of course never dug deep enough to find the truth. They even jumped in a helicopter to get a better look. Sorry to say, you will see nothing in a helicopter since the light does not come from the sky. It comes from car lights about 7.2 miles up the road on a path that is in line with the spot of where people are seeing the light. I am jumping ahead of myself. Let's get the folklore out of the way first.

### The Information we are given

The Paulding Light or sometimes called the "Dog Meadow Light" is a light that appears in a valley that lies outside of Paulding, Michigan. Reports of the light have appeared since the 1960s, with popular folklore providing such explanations as ghosts, geologic activity, or swamp gas.

In 2010, Syfy Channel's *Fact or Faked* conducted a paranormal investigation and concluded that the Paulding Light was unexplained. Michigan Tech students conducting a scientific investigation of the light in 2010 were able to see automobile headlights and tail lights when viewing the light through a telescope. They recreated the effect of the light by driving a car through a specific stretch of US Highway 45.

The first recorded sighting of the Paulding Light was in 1966, when a group of teenagers reported the light to a local sheriff. Since then, a number of other individuals have reported seeing the mysterious light.

Although stories related to the light vary, the most popular legend involves the death of a railroad brakeman. The legend states that the valley once contained railroad tracks. The light is the lantern of the brakeman who was killed while attempting to stop an oncoming train from colliding with railway cars stopped on the tracks. Another story claims the light is the ghost of a slain mail courier, while another says that it is the ghost of an Indian dancing on the power lines that run through the valley.

In 2010, students from the Michigan Tech chapter of the Society of Photo-Optical Instrumentation Engineers (SPIE) used a telescope to examine the light, and were able to clearly see vehicles and stationary objects on a highway, including a specific Adopt-a-Highway sign. They were reportedly able to recreate the Paulding Light by driving a car through a specific location on US 45. They also recreated other observations related to the light, such as multicolored patterns (police flashers) and variations in intensity (high and low beams). They theorized that the stability of an inversion layer allowed the lights to be visible from the stretch of Highway 45.

I have been to the Paulding Light many times, and while the light is not real and only a folklore, there are some other happenings that have happened to us while in the area. In the 90s, my mom had cancer and only had a few days left. My dad told me why don't I go hang out with my friends. I think he didn't want me to see her pass away as he knew her time was close. My friends took me up to the light to hang out. Beyond that fence in the above picture was a road that leads down to a creek. We walked down by the creek that night and heard a voice whisper close to us and we all heard it. I am not sure what it said, but something was there on the path with us. We hung out by the river for a while and then headed back up toward our cars. I heard something again behind me, and when I turned around, there was this big white light that came up to me and stopped for a few seconds, then shot upward and vanished. When I got home that night, I found out my mom had passed away and that it happened just after midnight. I was at the Paulding Light in the spot where I had seen the light around that time because I had looked at my watch. Could this have been my mom saying goodbye to me? I kind of hope so and believe that it was. I do regret not being there when she passed away, but she was so out of it, she would have not even known I was there. I would rather think that she came and saw me one last time.

It wasn't long after that time frame my best friend from Elkhorn, Charles Griffith, came up to visit me, and we decided to drive to the Paulding Light to check out the area. We found a road that goes to the left just before the fence and drove down there to see where we would end up. It went on for miles and miles and came to a spot where you could camp if you wanted to, although you would still have to get a permit. There was a mill pond there and a sign that said there was a former mill on the pond and basically states ghost-town and no longer there. We walked around for a bit to check the area out. It would be a place I would love to come back to and camp and was in the middle of no where. We headed back up the road back to the light area and parked by the fence, and it was quiet; no one else was there. We walked down toward the creek but would never make it to the creek. About half way down something big walked out of the woods in front of us and all we had was our phone, and if I remember right, there was no flashlight app on the phone. We could not see clearly what it was, but it was taller than me, and I am 5 foot 8, with Charles being slightly taller. It made a clicking noise and seemed very dark, almost black. It wasn't a bear, and I swear it was standing on its hind legs. We noticed one more thing before we ran the other way. It had green eyes and it wasn't a deer. The thing with the green eyes that bothers me today is, there was no light shining off the thing, so why did its eyes lit up? I will never know what it was and wouldn't mind checking the area out a little more sometime. I watched a movie many years later about the Mothman and it was based on a true story. Could that have been a Mothman or Bigfoot? We have no ideas to what it was, but Charles and I still talk about it to this day.

There are other anomalies in that area like photos that are out of focus and reports of weird animals. Some have captured people in photos who were not with them. I have captured EVPs on the trail there when it's quiet. I often wonder if it has something to do with the time zone change that is close to the light. Maybe it's something we will never figure out other than the lights.

Now I have been told by others the real light has not been seen in years or even decades. Now that is possible that maybe something long ago did create the spook light that follows your car. I always ask the people who tell me that how much they had to drink that night. I also have said on our Facebook page that if anyone can prove to me that it's paranormal and not car lights, I bet $300.00. I even offered $500.00 at one time to anyone who could take me there and show me something other than car lights.

If they lose, I get the money and I will donate it to make a wish foundation. No one ever wants to bet me but still try to tell me it's not car lights, even though it's been proven over and over again. Who is up for a good bet?

## September 2017 debunking of the light

We were visiting another haunted area, and I had brought what I needed to bring this time to debunk the light, which was a spotlight and two-way radios with 25 mile range. We also had another team with us as well to help out. I shot two videos to show people our findings, and you can find them on YouTube under "Paulding Light debunking day view" and "Paulding light debunked". One of the videos is shot during the day to show you where you can park to use spotlights, to show your friends you have become the light. The other is taken at night while we had people on one end where you see the light and at the other end where I had spot lights. We headed out to Robbins Pond Road where you are able to view the light. We had two cars, and Krista and Kara had the two-way radio and the voice recorder, and I had them stay on top of the hill where you could view the light. Jason and I drove to the other side close to a road called, Ericson Lake Road. It's about 7.2 miles further North on US Hwy 45. We got out of the car and called down to Kara and Krista. I told them I would turn on my red flashers, and I did, and they were able to see them. I told them I would pull out the spotlight to become the light and had them give me a sequence of on then off and so on. They were able to see the light plain as day and so did the people who showed up out there. Krista asked them to tell her when they saw the light. A girl called out to Krista and said, "There it is." Krista explained that it was my spotlight they were seeing and they were bummed out, but thought it was cool we were there to try to solve it. So when you see red, it's the taillights headed up the slope 7.2 miles away, and when you see the light, it's the headlights. The headlights from that distance make it look like it is only one light and the telephone poles line up with the viewpoint 7.2 miles away. There is a hill, so the light vanishes and then appears again when another car comes over the top of the hill. Even though this a tale we still like to go up and visit and see what other things we might see in the surrounding woods. I was able to talk to town officials after I had filmed the videos and they also stated that it is a fun thing to do and that it was fake. It's a small town and needs some tourism, so why not a spooklight?

# CHAPTER 10

# THE HAUNTED HILL HOUSE
# LEOPOLIS, WISCONSIN

The haunted house on the hill is what all the neighbors and town folk refer to it as. All of the investigations in this book have been out of state other than this one. I can't let such a sinister house like this not make it into this book, since we have had so much happen inside this house. I got a call from a former team member, John, who happens to live close by. He said he is friends with a real estate agent named Richard who owns this house and was trying to rent it, but was having problems because it was haunted. I contacted Richard about the house and asked him what was going on in the house. Richard had lots of very interesting stories to tell and another team had investigated it prior to us coming out to look at it. The other team captured an apparition of what they think was a small boy in the attic named Oscar. They were able to capture it on video moving down along the wall toward the stairs. We were excited to meet Richard.

## The history and stories behind the haunting

The house was built in 1928 by Albert Brunner, who raised pigs to help get through the depression. There was a ghost that came with the house right after it was built. They called the ghost Oscar, even though they really were unsure of its real name. There is really not too much history that goes along with this house. Albert later on in life became a Real Estate Broker. The house was also turned into assisted living for a while. It had a library of books that the town said they were proud of.

The stories behind the house told by Richard are as follows: They were cleaning out the house and getting it ready to rent. One of his friends found a bunch of antlers from some deer in the basement of the house. He removed them from the house and took them home. The next morning on returning to the house to do more cleaning, some odd things started to happen. Lights kept going on and off and flickering. Then out of the old radiators in the house, a loud growling could be heard. The heat was not on and the radiators were not in use, yet loud groaning and growling noises could be heard coming out of them from the basement. The cleaner called Richard and explained that after he took the antlers out of the basement, this was what was going on. Richard said, "Get those antlers back in the house at once." Once they were brought back in, the growling stopped, but the activity started to increase while remodeling. They would still have lights flickering and loud knocks and bangs. Some of them heard footsteps and saw shadows. One of the caretakers,

Shawn, who is taking care of the place, had turned off the light in his room only to have it come back on and then fade out. Richard told him that the electrical is old in the house and that this type of current makes the lights come back on after they are turned off. This really wasn't the case but was only said so Shawn was not creeped out while staying there. Richard will not spend the night alone in the house after dark. Richard who was friends with one of our former team members, John, who now helps us out from time to time, was with another team in the area that investigate this house. On their investigation, they had captured the shadow of the little boy that they thought could be Oscar up in the attic. They also captured lots of EVPs and disembodied voices as well. There is an old metal shed on the property of the house that John said they investigated. As they approached the shed and started to open the sliding door, a voice said, "Get the f*** out." They were able to hear this voice clearly without a voice recorder. They heard it a second time too. They opened the shed and nothing was in the shed other than some trash. Someone must not have liked them opening this shed. There is also a garage with what must have been some old living quarters above it at one point. Richard said there was a rumor that someone had hung himself or herself above this garage, but we are yet to confirm this. I asked Richard if we could come in and do an investigation, and of course he said yes, so the next week we headed out there.

I called John and told him to meet us out there so that he could give us a tour of where he got some evidence. It was Lisa, Jennifer, Drew, Andrea, and I on the investigation, and we had brought some sleeping bags to spend the night. We met with Richard and John. We all sat down in the dining room. Richard had bought this old dining-room table with these chairs that had backs on them that forced you to sit up straight. It was an old table and looking at it made you wonder if something could have been attached to the table. Richard and John said he would give us a tour of the place. There were two entrances to the place—a front door with a sidewalk leading down to the road and mailbox. You had to pass under a bunch of lilac bushes, and they were in full bloom. There was a back door with a little porch to grill out on. The garage with the loft sat back about 75 feet from the house, and the metal shed where they heard the voices was about 100 feet away. Further back on the property was an old barn that had fallen in on itself and there was really nothing left inside. There was quite a bit of property one could investigate there. I was not about to go roaming in the woods with the ticks. Inside the back door was a hallway that went onward to the kitchen on the right. There was a small bathroom as you walked through the back door and then one other door that led downstairs. Next to the kitchen was the dining room and a small living room with a fireplace that once housed the really nice library. We headed downstairs to a couple different rooms. There was one to the right that had the hot water heater and a few more off the main section of the basement that had no windows inside. I thought possibly an old pantry where they stored jars of canned goods. The furnace was in pieces as they were working on it. We headed upstairs to the second floor. There were three bedrooms and one had an old hospital bed that Richard had picked up and placed in the bedroom. There was a bathroom on this floor as well. There was a hallway outside of the two bedrooms that had one more door that led up to the attic. On the way up to the attic, John showed us the first step which lifted up and had a chute all the way to the basement which was the laundry chute. Once up in the attic, I could stand all the way up in the middle, but the sides were slanted, and I had to duck in those spots. It looked as though there was once a bedroom up here. The radiator sat in the middle of the floor and a spot where a wall once was. Now it was just a wide open attic with some drawings of dogs on the ceiling, possibly done by some kids. There was also little plastic beads on the floor. I noticed two doorways built into the attic wall for extra storage. They were warped and hard to open, but I managed to get them open, and the only thing inside now was insulation. There was an attic space above the attic with nothing inside as well. We all headed back down to the dining room table to take a break before getting started. While sitting and talking at the table, we heard footsteps come down the stairs from the second floor and stop right outside the doors leading out of the dining room. We all heard them, and I told John to get up and walk over to the door and open it up. Just as he grabbed the door knob, the ghost ran back up the stairs and across the second floor and it was loud. We went upstairs and found nothing but an empty room.

Our next stop was downstairs to investigate down there. We sat in the darkness and it suddenly got very cold. The entrance that we came through blacked out as if someone was standing there. We had a Rem-Pod at the top of the stairs and that was going off to let us know that something was indeed there. It became quiet and the meters stopped going off. We all walked over to one of the rooms I thought was used for canning. We stood in there for a little while, and we all thought we heard a groan followed by this crazy bright white light that shot past John and up into the ceiling and was gone. Only some of us saw the light, but everyone heard the groan. We headed upstairs from there to the attic. Richard and John said this would be their last stop before leaving us there for the night. We all sat up in the attic and were asking questions, when suddenly something was tossed into the middle of the room. It bounced a couple times before coming to a stop. I shined the flashlight, but the only thing I could see where the beads on the floor, and it's very possible it was any one of the beads lying there that was tossed. I knocked three times and something knocked back three times in return very close to where I was sitting. We sat up there for about an hour doing some recordings and then headed downstairs to say goodbye to John and Richard who were heading out and leaving us behind to investigate some more. We wanted to head outside for a bit to check out the shed where the other team had captured a voice that said get out. We opened the shed but heard was nothing. Inside the shed was some trash dated only a couple months ago and what looked like an old pillow and jacket. It looked to me like someone was squatting in here at some point. We asked a couple questions and headed to check out the loft-type room above the garage where someone was said to have committed suicide. We peeked inside and it was quite hot up there and there were tons of bat crap laying in the corners. There was also some raccoon droppings close to the walls. We did not hear anything at all up here, but the smell was bad, so we didn't stay long. We headed back into the house up to the attic to check that out some more. Drew said he felt like something touched him and Lisa and Jennifer were feeling some cold drafts. I pulled out the Ghost-box and was asking who was there with us. We heard the name Heather come through about seven times on there. The activity slowed down so we thought we try downstairs one last time. The Rem-Pod went off again at the top of the stairs like something was playing with it and more cold spots all around us. There was a loud dragging noise of something metal that came from very close to us in the basement, but nothing could be seen. We decided it was time to get some rest, and went to the dining room to set up our sleeping bags. We slept most of the night without anything other than some footsteps here and there that seemed to come up and down the stairs from the second floor. I called Richard the next day and told him we had a great time. I said we would love to do some tours here for guests since the house was not rented. He said that he would be happy to have us. We now offer tours and over-nights here for guests and other teams.

The next couple days I had time to go over the voice recorder from our investigation. In the attic I captured a voice of a little girl saying, "I am in the classroom." Now we have no clue that this was any type of school or a class-room, but we don't know for sure. We don't know what was here before the house. There is a church next door and a cemetery close by. I also captured a voice saying, "Two men buried out back on property." Now being that the cemetery was close by and some of the rumors are that the graves were relo-cated. There was also a period of time when loved ones were able to bury the dead on their own property as well. One more review of the audio above the garage, we captured a voice saying its name was Casper. The last voice was captured by the shed when we were inside looking at the junk on the floor. There was a distinct male voice that said, "Get the f*** out of my shed." This would be the same voice that the other team captured months before. A guest on a recent tour went out to the shed while we were inside and taunted the ghost in the shed. We don't allow taunting of ghosts but are not able to see what our guests do when we are not around. They brought it to my attention because after the investigation he was taken to the hospital with a terrible headache. He stated he never had a headache like this before and was worried it was because he had called the ghost out in the shed. I have no answers for this or if it was because of his actions, but who knows.

I called on a friend of mine, Becky Jo, who is a Psychic Medium and asked if she wanted to check the house out and see what she might find by going there.

She showed up about a week later and met us out by the house before one of our scheduled tours. After her findings of the house, she told us that she sensed there were quite a few people and animals buried on the property. None of the ghosts were negative or harmful, although one was mischievous and liked to poke fun at the guests or investigators. Now even the normal everyday ghost or spirit can move objects and even scratch you if they want. That still don't make them demonic like some people think. Becky Jo also said that she believes there are some kids that still play on the property and in the house. We have captured many voices of the little girl in the attic and other locations of the house. We still have the name Heather floating around this location but are uncertain if she is the little girl. A native of Leopolis has told Richard that there was a woman that lived in the house named Heather, but we think she is still living. Becky was able to help Richard understand more of what was in the house and that nothing was going to harm him. We have investigated this house many times since she has been there. We have not encountered anything evil, but some of our investigators have left the basement area in recent weeks in tears saying something was not quite right down there. They felt like something was watching them and that it was very cold and the dark kept getting darker around them. I have felt the cold spots but not the feeling of dread like they have.

**The most recent tours in July 2018**

We had a call from some guests that wanted to book 3 hours for an investigation. I called on Drew and John to come help out on the investigation. We all arrived about an hour early to make sure everything is cleaned up in the house. There is still some remodeling going on in the house, so we have to make sure it's safe for the guests. Guests were arriving and it was just getting dark outside. John walked around with a thermal camera to see if he could capture anything on the camera. He caught something in the kitchen and showed Drew the picture. It looked like a person standing in the kitchen near the sink. There was a bright spot that we debunked as being a reflection off the sink, but the person standing there was not. We could not find anything that could have created the person standing in the kitchen. Sometimes one can get a reflection off the window while taking pictures, but there were no windows close to where the person was caught.

Craig, Drew, and John before the investigation

All the guests were there now including Steven who had a Go-Pro and some other equipment with him to make video on the tour. We hung out in the main dining area for a while asking questions. We heard what sounded like a scream come from somewhere in the house. We also thought we heard some growls but was debunked. It was the wind blowing through an air unit in the wall. We closed that up and continued to investigate and ask more questions. We again heard the scream only this time, and it was followed by a loud bang upstairs. We were the only ones in the house, so what was upstairs? Drew said he thought he felt something touch his elbow. We decided to head up to the second floor and heard a loud voice as we came around the corner to the staircase. I reviewed audio on the recorder first and found a voice that said, "Here they come." I assume that meant they knew we were headed to the second floor. We continued onto the attic to spend some time asking questions up there.

Like some of the last tours we had, there were more of the plastic beads that were tossed toward us. One landed next to me, and I flipped the flashlight on. It was a red bead that was not there before when I had sat down. We heard another one bounce off the wall and down the stairs, yet nothing could be seen in the room. There was something sitting next to Drew or at least that is what he thought since it was getting icy cold and it was 80 degrees in the attic. We were dying from the heat up there, so we headed to the basement since it's cooler down there. We spread out so that we were in different areas and rooms. We heard a loud noise like metal on metal pipes right behind us. The girls on the tour jumped and ran to each other and decided that was a good place to stay. The light blocked out at the top of the staircase and the Rem-Pod went off in short bursts of light to show something was there and touching it. The first part of the tour was done and some of the guests had to leave. John said he had to duck out to get home for the night. I still had Drew with me, so that was not a problem. We took a short break before starting in the dining room.

We all sat around the dining room table, and I set the Rem-Pod just outside the room by the stairs. We were chatting about the caretakers dog that ran away, when suddenly the Rem started to go off, and not just one light but all the lights, which meant something was not just standing there but grabbing on to it. While the pod was going off, we heard something coming down the stairs and it stopped just in front of us. I got goose bumps and all my hair stood on end. Everyone else in the room felt the same way and it seemed colder. We sat quietly and heard something moving just outside of the dining area close to the pod. I decided I would walk out there and see if I could see anything or if it would run the other way. It didn't run the other way, but stood its ground and grabbed my side with its hand. I felt the full hand with fingers go around my waist which made me jump, and I let out a yelp, as I backed up quickly back into the room to sit down. I have not felt a whole hand on me in a long time. Drew thought he would go out there and check it out and also had something touch his shoulder. Steven who was filming and his friend came out into the hallway to see if they could hear or feel anything. Nothing else came in the form of fingers or hands on us, but noise now continued on the staircase. We heard footsteps on the staircase and some loud noises from the above rooms somewhere. We decided to head upstairs to see what we could find.

We stopped for a session of questions in the room where Richard had put the hospital bed he bought. It was also stated that Oscar liked this room as well. We asked some more questions and then turned the Ghost Box on and something said we should go into the basement. That was fine with us since it was still very hot upstairs. We got to the basement and spread out into different rooms. I sat on the stairs and Drew was against the wall in front of me. I felt a blast of cold air shoot past me and Drew caught the tail end of the breeze. I said, "What the hell was that?" We heard a long loud groan from the top floor like the house just came to life. It freaked us all out. We all knew there was only one way out and that was up the stairs, but we were not going to be scared away. We stood our ground and other than some scraping noises upstairs all became very quiet. Maybe they all went to bed. We headed back upstairs to the dining room and hung out for a while before all the guests were gone. We closed up and locked everything up. We have had some teams in there since that have captured shadows in the basement while using the Ghost-grid, a laser device that shines a bunch of little green lights or whatever color you shine onto the wall. When something crosses the path of the green lights, it blacks out or casts a shadow on the wall of lights. In the next weeks, I had a chance to go over all the audio from that night of our investigations of me being grabbed and some of the voices are as follows:

"Craig is here"
"Polo" – which was the answer to me yelling "Marko"
"Anne is here"
"Something is up here with us" - This came from the attic
"Mom and Debbie hate this"
"Time for bed"
"Yes, three men dead in backyard"
"Touch it now" – In response to me asking to touch Rem-Pod

While we were investigating in the room with the hospital bed, we captured girls laughing that sounded like it was coming from the stairs.

We continue to investigate this house and will be allowing teams and tours in the house until it is rented. We always offer free investgations, for our clients who have houses or a business with paranormal activity.

# CHAPTER 11

# St Albans Sanatorium
# Radford, Virginia

St Albans was a place that I saw listed on some links that popped up where teams can spend the night. I noticed that it was huge and had lots of floors to investigate. I called and got hold of Marcelle and scheduled two nights in July with one of the days falling on Friday the 13th. Our team was looking forward to this one because it's the furthest we would be traveling for an investigation, all the way to Virginia.

## The History

During the 1700s, the city's close proximity to the New River Watershed attracted Native Americans and early European settlers. Competition over the area resulted in hostilities between the two groups. In July 1755, a group of Shawnee Indians attacked and looted the colonists of Draper's Meadow, killing at least five people and taking others as hostage. Shawnee left behind grisly reminders of their wrath. A bag containing the decapitated head of Philip Barger.

Mary Draper Ingles was one of those held for ransom at the Shawnee town of Sonnontio. Before she was taken prisoner, Mary first had to witness the gruesome deaths of her fellow colonists, including her mother and sister-in-law's baby.

Eleanor Draper was tomahawked and scalped. Betty Draper's infant child was brained against the side of one of the cabins. Mary eventually managed to escape from Sonnontio.

Drapers Meadow Massacre are the first to contribute to St. Albans Sanatorium's scary past. Next are what soldiers endured during one of the Civil War's most violent battles, the Battle of Cloyd's Mountain. According to St. Albans, "Union artillery bombarded the settlement of Central Depot from the ridge where St. Albans stands today. Many people who have visited the building report of hearing rifle shots, smelling gun smoke, and seeing mists rise from the hospital's surrounding grounds.

St. Albans Sanatorium was constructed in 1892, though it first functioned as a Lutheran Boys School. As Headmaster, Miles demanded boys to perform well in classrooms and on sports fields. To meet such high expectations, many would turn to extreme methods. St. Albans thus "quickly developed a reputation for being a rough and competitive school where bullying was not only condoned, it was encouraged." Heated athletic rivalries may have allowed St. Albans to secure numerous football championships, but also made homicides and suicides frequent occurrences.

After Miles' death in 1903, enrollment at St. Albans quickly fell, and closed eight years later. In 1916, Dr. John C. King acquired the property to fulfill a vision: introducing the nation's first top-notch psychiatric hospital. Dr. King wanted to open an institution where patients would be both well treated and well accommodated. He made several renovations to the school's remnants, even adding a farm to the property in order to give patients a proper place to exercise.

The history of psychiatric treatment methods during the 1900s is a story of failures replacing failures. Insulin-induced comas and lobotomies would leave patients either brain dead, for example. These procedures were also very labor intensive, and St. Albans staff-to-patient ratio in 1945 was a sad 48 to 6509.

When cutting people's skulls open proved ineffective, doctors opted to simply shock them to their senses. Schizophrenics, for instance, were given electroconvulsive therapy, which was deemed safer than insulin coma therapy.

Some of St. Albans Sanatorium's most active rooms are where hydrotherapies were conducted. A hydrotherapy session didn't always involve a relaxing soak in the bathtub. Patients who weren't mummified in icy cold towels were strapped into steaming water vats. Others were hit with cold water. One of these rooms is now known as the Suicide Bathroom.

The Bowling Alley in the basement, for instance, is known to be haunted by two female spirits: "Allie" and "Gina Renee Hall". Allie is rumored to be the young daughter of one of the hospital's patients, and Gina was a woman who was murdered on June 28, 1980, somewhere close to St. Albans Sanatorium.

In the 1990s, the Carilion Health System acquired St. Albans Sanatorium, but vacated the property in 2003. Tim Gregory, a previous patient at the hospital acquired the hospital and became the new owner; he made it his mission to renovate its remaining buildings and transform it into a research center. Today, to fund these efforts, he hosts a number of events at St. Albans Sanatorium, including an annual Haunted House Halloween extravaganza. As guests roam through the building, they encounter zombies and mental patients, but can't always be sure if they are staged or real.

There are many ghosts of St. Albans and my suggestion would be to pick up a book on this link that explains the ghosts in great detail and it's called The Ghosts Of St. Albans Sanatorium www.stalbans-sanatorium.com/the-ghosts-of-st-albans-sanatorium/

It was a long trip down to Radford for us and we booked these really neat cabins on a river. The cabins were called Walker Creek Cabins and just add a .com after it to find them when you go to visit. We had the Barefoot Cabin which should have been called the loudfoot cabin. Our experiences in this cabin were almost as remarkable as the investigation was at St. Albans and for some of us more intense. We had five investigators in that cabin and the others were in the Creekside Cabin. Our first night at Barefoot Cabin, we had Jennifer, Lisa, and Jason up in the loft and I was down in the back bedroom. It started with a light that kept going on and off for no apparent reason and we checked the switches and they were in the off mode. Well, that happened for about half of an hour and then it stopped. We all tried to get some sleep so we could enjoy the next day. I heard three loud knocks but figured it was just them upstairs in the loft. I also thought it might have been Lauralye since she left for the night with a guy friend of hers that happened to be in the area. I know she called and said she was spending the night with him but thought maybe she came back early. Suddenly there were three more loud knocks and Radio yelled down to me and said, "Craig, is that you." I said, "No." Drew came down the stairs and opened the front door to find no one there. We were a little freaked out to say the least since we were a ways out of town and the only ones in this cabin, as the others were not arriving till the next day. The cabins sit in a valley between two high hills and a river runs by. The one other cabin that was there had no guests in it. Drew grabbed some object and ran further into the darkness to see if he could see anything, yet no one was there. There were no noises outside, yet we all clearly heard six loud knocks. We locked the doors and went to sleep with no further incidents. Lauralye arrived back at the cabin early the next morning and we told her all that had happened. We had a full day to blow before the investigation and the other investigators that were on there way down. Some of them were running behind because they stopped at the Mothman Museum in Point Pleasant, West Virginia. We had stopped there the day before as well. *The Mothman Prophecies*, also a major motion picture is based on true events from 1966. We decided to hit up a waterfall called the Cascades about 15 min from the cabins.

I seem to always manage to do myself in prior to investigations and today would be no different. We got to the base of the mountain that would take us on a two-mile trek up to the waterfall. That's not so bad, I thought to myself. One mile in, and I wanted to pass out, not just from the heat, but if there was a zombie apocalypse, I would be eaten alive from lack of cardio. The rest of the team left me so far behind that I would be easy picking for the bears in the area. I was lucky I had Lauralye coaching me saying, "It's not much farther." A half mile later, I found myself asking the other hikers how far it was yet, and the answer was, you're getting closer and you wont regret it. It wouldn't have been so bad, but it was all uphill. I finally made it to a sign that said "waterfall below". It was all that it was supposed to be and worth walking there. I was so hot that I had to jump in and cool off by the falls. We stopped long enough to take a picture and tell a guy who was on top of the falls trying to take a running start to jump over the rocks not to do it. He would not have made it and he changed his mind as well. I was told many have drowned there.

Cascade Falls – Jennifer, Craig, Drew, Lisa, and Jason

I just remembered I had two miles back down the mountain. I thought this would be easier, and it was, but my knees were starting to bother me to the point I started to limp. I eventually made it to the bottom coming in last like the turtle in the race. We headed back to the cabin and met with Jay and Kerri who made it to Creekside Cabin and was taking a nap from the drive. Soon Krista, Adam, and Kara would be there and we would cookout before heading to St. Albans for the first night of investigations.

## St. Albans first night of the investigation

We arrived at St. Albans and met up with our tour guide that would be showing us around for the night. After a quick tour with very little history or even telling us where stuff happened, we were let loose on our end. The staff told us if we get lost, to radio them on some radios that they handed out to us, or if we needed to find a certain location that was shown to us on the tour. We had 11 investigators, so I sent 3 groups out in certain directions to investigate. I joined Jason and Jay in one of the waiting room to electroshock therapy. We all sat about 10 feet apart from each other and turned off the lights. It was so dark that you were unable to see your hand in front of your face. We sat there for a little while and Jason was asking questions when we all heard a disembodied voice and it sounded like a little girl. We heard a couple more voices but couldn't make out what they said. It got quiet and nothing more was heard, so we headed back out to the break room to see if anyone else had any luck. Lisa and Jennifer said they were in Donald's room where all the toys were. They said the Rem-Pod was going off and some other noises were being heard. Kerri, Krista, Drew, Adam, and Lauralye were down in the bowling alley but all was quiet. They also checked out the boiler room, but all they heard was water coming down the pipes when someone flushed the toilet upstairs.

It was round two and I wanted to check out Donald's room with Lisa and Jennifer, so we headed up there. I started by asking questions to see if Donald was there. I asked him to touch the Rem-Pod and the pod started going off like crazy. It stopped and we sat in silence just listening to everything around us. All of a sudden we hear this loud noise followed by a swoosh and something rubbing on something. We walked out into the hallway and found one of the air ducts that was in the ceiling that was firmly attached there had fallen down and was swinging back and forth. I was curious to if this was paranormal or if the movement from the people walking around in the attic caused the air duct to fall. I had the investigators in the attic jump around a little bit but could not get anything to move around at all. We had no explanation of the duct falling and I happened to be talking about Donald at the time. We moved out to the hallway to see if we could hear anything out in the hall. We heard a couple knocks and bangs, but nothing more. We stopped to take a picture of a huge Wolf Spider in one of the stairwells. We headed back down to the breakroom. I met with Drew and he said he was down in Isolation and something had touched him while sitting in the room. Krista and Kara had something poke them in the attic while we were in Donald's room. Kara also said that it had followed her from room to room. Krista saw a shadow in the room that she thought might have been following Kara. She put a K2 in the room to try to get the shadow person to communicate. It left after she set the K2 down.

The next hour Jay and I headed down to the salon where they would cut hair of the people residing at the Sanatorium. The wall had floral wallpaper and had none of the equipment there at all, just an empty room. The room was below the stairwell and another room used for storage now was across from it. They said that was the original file room for all the people that stayed there. We asked, who was there, and two voices came out of the dark, but again we were unable to figure out what they said. I knocked three times and another loud knock came back from the closet. There was nothing in the closet at all when we checked. We headed back upstairs, and with all the stairs we had to climb, I was in some pain from the long walk to the waterfall earlier that day.

We all met back in break area and it was about midnight. We relaxed for a little while but wanted to get our monies worth. Our plans were to stay till about 2 a.m., plus we had an hour drive back to the cabin where we were staying at.

Our break was done and Drew and I headed down to the bowling alley. We sat down there for a while, but nothing was heard. I would have heard a pin fall to the ground since that is how quiet it was. We checked out the boiler room but heard the water in the pipes. We left the boiler room and headed down to Isolation where he was touched a few hours earlier. I thought something pulled my pants leg while I was sitting there but wasn't sure. It never happened again and all was quiet. We headed back upstairs to see how the others were doing. The rest of the team was tired and wanted to head back to the cabins. We had one more night, so some rest would be nice. Nothing happened at our cabin that night that I recall; however, I was so tired I wouldn't have noticed anyways.

The next day we woke up and enjoyed fishing and tubing on the river in front of the cabins. Jennifer noticed a huge black snake which I found was not poisonous. It went under Drew's car and never came out the other side. When we looked under the car it was not there. Drew backed the car up and it was still not there. So we are still not sure what happened to the snake or was it a ghost snake?.

## St. Albans night two investigations

The team in front of St. Albans Sanatorium

We arrived early to St. Albans to take some pictures before dark inside and outside the building. We all then started in the break room and split into groups to investigate. Jay, Kerri, and I headed down to the waiting room of the shock therapy to see if we might hear what we heard the night before. We only stayed about half hour in that spot and nothing happened in that area so we moved on. We headed downstairs to the bowling alley but encountered Jennifer and Lisa. We didn't want to disturb them, so we headed upstairs to see what we could find. We heard a few noises but nothing really interesting. Jay said he wanted Starbucks to stay awake, so we headed to the break room to see who wanted some coffee. Jay and Jason went out on a run to get the coffee and it seemed like it was forever and a day for them to get back. They called and said they got pulled over by the police. The police were pulling cars over and giving people sobriety tests. They were not drinking and had nothing to worry about, but that took them a long time.

Once refreshed we headed to the attic and ran into Adam, Krista, and Drew, who left to investigate before us. They were talking to someone that they could not see in the suicide bathroom where a couple people have taken their lives while residing there. They were getting noises and loud knocks. It must not have liked us coming up as everything got quiet. It was really hot up there, and Drew, Adam and Krista left the area to cool off. I stayed up there with Jennifer, Jay, and Lisa. Jay set the Rem-Pod in the suicide bathroom. It wasn't long and the pod was going off to Jay asking questions. I was leaning against a wall and it felt like something jabbed me with a pin in my shoulder. I thought something scratched me. I had Jennifer check my back and she found a bug on my shoulder that very well have been the culprit that bit me. Jay asked if the ghost liked me and the pod stayed quiet. He then asked if the ghost didn't want me there and the pod lit up like crazy. I moved from the wall and walked over and sat where I could get a better view. I asked the ghost to light it up if it didn't like me and the pod went off like crazy. Jay said if you light it up one more time on the count of 5, then I would leave the room. He counted up to 5, and when he said 5 the pod lit up like crazy. I eventually left and they had more activity. I am not sure why the ghost in the suicide bath-room wasn't fond of me. I came back down to the break room to see Krista and see if anything happened to them in the attic. Krista said a little child had grabbed her hand while up in the attic. Kerri and Lauralye came back from the waiting room of shock therapy and said they were talking to a little girl who said her name was Olivia. My Ghost-Box sessions were very quiet. I normally get quite a bit on my Ghost-Box, but I caught very little while there. Kerri also said that Olivia was answering questions with the Mel-Meter.

Kerri took this picture of an old wheelchair

We all headed off in different directions to check out rooms one last time. I checked out the bowling alley one last time with Drew, but captured nothing. I took some pics of the old Brunswick pin setters and we headed back upstairs. Everyone else was rather tired and wanted to call it a night. We thanked the tour guides and headed back to the cabins.

Once back to our cabin, stuff started to happen again. Jayson decided to stay the night with us because of all the things going on there. We were all in bed when we heard loud footsteps out on the front porch. Jennifer, Lisa, Drew, and Lauralye were up in the loft and they heard them too. Jason was on the couch and yelled to me to come out of the back bedroom. Jennifer slowly walked down the stairs from the loft. The footsteps were coming from outside on the porch. Jennifer looked outside and saw the swing on the porch swinging back and forth. I looked out as well, and as soon as I did, the swing stopped. There was no wind outside and the swing don't move unless you are sitting in it. We were all a little freaked out, since whatever was walking around out there was of the paranormal ghost kind. I headed back to the bedroom to look out the window since it was above the porch. I saw a shadow move past the window with a tall brim hat on, possibly like a Civil war soldier. I remembered talking with the owner of the cabins and she said another guest reported Civil war soldier walking up the driveway of one of the cabins a couple years back. I ran back out of the room to tell everyone, and we all looked outside. There was nothing out there. Once back inside, the lights kept going on and off like they did the first night and then all was quiet.

Barefoot cabin with all the activity.

# EQUIPMENT

### Voice recorders
We use all types of voice recorders from Sony to RCA. They capture the Electronic Voice Phenomenon (EVPs). They are the most important piece of equipment on an investigation.

### K2 Meters
This K2 meter is a easy-to-use tool that detects spikes in electromagnetic energy. These spikes indicated by the multicolor lights at the top of the meter may signify activity or communication from spirits from the other side.

### Mel-Meter
The Mel Meter is an intelligent microprocessor-based instrument specifically designed for paranormal investigators. The Mel Meter incorporates various features that are combined into a durable unit designed to be operated with only one hand. First and foremost, the Mel Meter is the only instrument on the market to be able to record EMF and Temperature simultaneously.

### Rem-Pod
Rem-Pod uses a mini telescopic antenna to radiate its own independent magnetic field around the instrument. This EM field can be easily influenced

by materials and objects that conduct electricity. Based on source proximity, strength, and EM field distortion, colorful LED lights can be activated in any order or combination. The Rem-Pod is intended to further help promote and advance Paranormal research.

### DVR & Cameras

We also run a DVR which in most aspects is used as security. We use it to record 4 different areas with 4 cameras that have night vision in total darkness. We are able to set cameras up in certain rooms that have activity. The DVR can record up to 365 days at a time, after that it will record over the old data. I can also set it up to only record motion.

### Thermal Camera

Thermal imaging cameras have always been a popular tool with ghost hunters. Ghost hunters are interested in the technology behind thermal cameras as it allows them to visualize the heat of an area. It is widely believed that paranormal activity can cause an influence on the heat of objects, which is why ghost hunters use the cameras as an analysis tool.

### Go Pro Full Spectrum Camcorder

This camcorder takes full spectrum video that you can mount anywhere. This camcorder has been professionally modified with UV and IR sensitivity to view the full spectrum of light including light not seen with the human eye. This helps with Ghost-Hunting because you can mount it to your chest or headband and walk around corners and capture everything in total darkness.

Where do we buy this equipment? Check the links below.

www.ghoststop.com

www.theghosthunterstore.com

www.amazon.com

## Current Team Members
Craig Nehring - Founder / Case Manager
Lyle Noss - Investigator
Lloyd Noss - Investigator
Lynzi Marie - Investigator
Shannon Schultz - Investigator
Haley Eyestone - Investigator

## Investigators that are listed in this book

| | |
|---|---|
| Jason Boone | Jeremy James |
| Don Bruechert | Brandon Kramer |
| John Butschli | Miranda Lee |
| Katie Brietzke | Adam Michael |
| Lori Ceman | Jodi Mazola |
| Jordan Drummond | Lauralye Rollins |
| Vanessa Forqurean | Jessica Timm |
| Sheila Hietpas | Michelle Le Clair |
| Julia Hebbe | Tia Vang |
| Trina Herlache | Rick Seefeldt |
| Daphne Ferren | Sunshine Warren |
| MJ | Charles Griffith |
| Jennifer Straw | Lisa Straw |
| Drew Kluesner | Jason Ehrhardt |
| Kara Burclaw | Jason Jameson |
| Kerri Jameson | |

## Information
Fox Valley Ghost Hunters on Facebook
Fox Valley Ghost Hunters on Youtube
foxvalleyghosthunters.com
team_fvgh@yahoo.com

Made in the USA
Monee, IL
24 October 2020

45787482R00073